The Greatest Champions of The WrestleMania Era

By "The Doc" Chad Matthews

This book is dedicated to my column readers around the world. In a strange way, those of us that become pen pals through our mutual appreciation for professional wrestling have become a family. Just as I navigate the waters of real life with my wife and kids, I ride the rollercoaster that is sports entertainment fandom with my wrestling family. Cheers!

DPC Publishing, Incorporated
North Carolina

"The Doc" Chad Matthews
The Greatest Champions Of The WrestleMania Era

ISBN-10: 0692579710

Editor: Corwin Metcalf
Cover Image: Chad Matthews

Contact

Chad Matthews is very active on social media, posting daily questions to wrestling fans on various topics to stimulate engaging debates.

To contact "The Doc" :

Twitter: @TheDocLOP

Facebook: https://www.facebook.com/doc.lop.9

Columns by "The Doc" Chad Matthews can be found on:

www.wrestlingheadlines.com / www.lordsofpain.net

To listen to "The Doc Says..." weekly podcast, please visit www.blogtalkradio.com/lordsofpain

Books by "The Doc" Chad Matthews

The WrestleMania Era: The Book of Sports Entertainment

Starrcade vs. WrestleMania: The Prelude to the Monday Night Wars (e-book)

The Greatest Matches, Rivalries, & Stories of the WrestleMania Era (estimated release in 2018)

Introduction

When I first embarked on getting *The WrestleMania Era: The Book of Sports Entertainment* published, I learned that a certain amount of brevity in the non-fiction literary world was greatly appreciated. Having always generally resonated with such writer-centric adages as "less is more" and "make your words count" and having applied those themes to most of my columns over the years, it should not have been difficult for me to transfer that mindset to my initial foray into booking writing.

I get a kick out of that now considering that the first draft was over 800 pages. The final product, at 594 pages, is still epically long for a generation of shorter attention spans, but some details of my analytical process to definitively name the Top 90 wrestlers since *Starrcade '83* had to be edited out. Among the deleted minutiae was a breakdown to accompany the statistical pages which largely helped make the decision for Wrestler A to be ranked ahead of Wrestler B. The bios on the wrestlers that made the cut, then, became more about paying tribute and less about the reasoning behind their rankings.

Earlier this year, I was approached about expanding *The WrestleMania Era* into a series of books, with the sequels to the original allowing me to feature a statistical analysis of each of the five-tiers that shaped the definitive list. The categories included a formula (to bridge the gap between eras) for championships won, a scale for main-events and headlining matches to account for longevity, a compilation of television ratings and pay-per-view buy rate data for box office success, a wrestler scoring system to reflect physical attributes and microphone skills, and a film critic-like star rating scale to account for performance. This book focuses on shaping the historical context around championship success.

Tangible accolades are a hallmark of any sport or entertainment avenue. The NBA has the Larry O'Brien trophy, the MVP, and the Defensive Player of the Year. Hollywood has the Oscar, the Golden Globe, and the Screen Actors Guild award. Professional wrestling has championship belts. Generally, there is not a more important role in the wrestling industry than being the World Champion. When a wrestler reaches that pinnacle, he becomes a face of the brand. The only higher honor to achieve in wrestling is to be in the main-event at WrestleMania. So, it is an important endeavor for establishing a hierarchy among wrestlers to create a systematic formula for championship glory.

In the old days, being the champion often meant wearing the gold around your waist for a year or longer. That has happened just twice in the last eighteen years. Title changes occurred more frequently beginning in the early 1990s and hit arguably ridiculous proportions during the Attitude Era. Thus, a yearlong-plus title reign from pre-1991 must be weighed against the 1992-present title reigns which have been much shorter. It is not fair for Sheamus's three reigns as a World Champ that lasted a combined 10 months, for example, to be given more credence than the single, 10-month title reign that Ultimate Warrior had from 1990-1991.

Credit must also be given where it is due to the secondary titleholders. Championships such as the Intercontinental, United States, and Tag Team titles have held various degrees of importance over the years, with the creative effort put into their respective divisions often waning from year-to-year (particularly since the Attitude Era), but they have also been stepping stones for future World Champions. Twenty-three of the top thirty stars of the WrestleMania Era held mid-card titles before becoming main-eventers.

Care had to be taken for the sake of accurate historical context not to allow more credit to be given for holding multiple titles in multiple divisions. For instance, Booker T held nearly thirty titles in his career, but that should not make him a greater champion than Hulk Hogan, who held just thirteen but spent virtually his entire career as a World Champion. Thus, each division was weighted according to its importance; the World Championship received top billing, beneath it the IC and US Titles were considered as equals followed by the Tag Team Titles. Belts such as the Cruiserweight, European, and Hardcore Championships were not taken into account because they were all short-lived; the major titles have been around throughout every period of the WrestleMania Era. For this reason, NWA Champions crowned after the WCW Championship became Ted Turner's #1 wrestling prize were not counted either.

The "Title Formula" was created to assess the championship resumes of all relevant WWE and WCW wrestlers between November 1983 and August 2015. In addition to its aforementioned emphasis on the pecking order, the formula also accounts for the length of reigns versus the number of reigns, giving maximum credit to Hogan and Ric Flair, each of whom had single World Championship reigns of over 500 days. The formula breaks down as follows:

(3 pts for being World Champion) X [(# of reigns of 119 days or fewer X 1) + (# of reigns of 120 days or greater X 2) + (# of reigns of 270 days or more X 3) + (# of reigns of 540 days or more X 4)]

+

(2 pts for being IC/US Champion) X [(# of reigns of 119 days or fewer X 1) + (# of reigns of 120 days or greater X 2) + (# of reigns of 210 days or more X 3) + (# of reigns of 300 days or more X 4)]

+

(1 pt for being Tag Team Champion) X [(# of reigns of 119 days or fewer X 1) + (# of reigns of 120 days or greater X 2) + (# of reigns of 210 days or more X 3) + (# of reigns of 300 days or more X 4)]

#200: Larry Zbyszko
1-time WCW Tag Team Champion

We begin with Hall of Famer Larry Zbyszko. If you had taken a poll of "smart" wrestling fans in their group-infancy back in May 1996 (before The New World Order was formed), then I am quite certain that the "Faction of the Decade" for the 1990s, to that point, would have been The Dangerous Alliance. While not the most famous member of the stable, Zbyszko had perhaps the best list of credentials of them all, but that list pre-dated the WrestleMania Era, unfairly labeling him as the weakest link in a group otherwise full of *WrestleMania Era* Top 90 talents. Zbyszko's tag team with Arn Anderson won the WCW gold in 1991. He had won the equivalent championship in WWE a decade prior, but he was a lot like Roddy Piper from that period in that he was not above the various titles, he just did not need them.

#199: Haku
1-time WWE Tag Team Champion

I grew up watching WWE in the late 1980s and beyond, so the ring announcer whose voice I hear in my head introducing any wrestler, past or present, is Howard Finkel. There are certain Finkel intros that stand out above the rest – Andre, Million Dollar Man, Hogan, Austin, etc. Haku is one of the most obscure names on that list for me, along with Haku's former partner, The Barbarian. As I sit here now, I can hear the enunciation echoing in my mind. Haku was, of course, the wrestler paired with Andre for the Giant's final days in the ring. They won the Tag Team Championships from Demolition in 1989 and dropped them back at WrestleMania VI.

#198: The Godwinns
2-time WWE Tag Team Champions

Whereas Haku won the Tag Team Titles during one of the Golden Ages of tag wrestling in WWE, Henry O. and Phineas I. Godwinn captured the straps twice in an era in which WWE was mightily struggling in the talent depth department. The Tag division has been at its best in WWE lore when the roster was stacked and the creative staff had to find ways to utilize it. The Godwinns and their completely forgettable two reigns for a whopping 9 days as champions emphasized how far the belts had fallen as compared to their late 1980's heights.

#197: Perry Saturn
2-time WCW Tag Team Champion

Though Perry Saturn won the WCW Tag Team Championships on a pair of occasions, he was never quite able to capture in World Championship Wrestling the same tag team mojo that he had in Extreme Championship Wrestling as one half of the Eliminators – one of the best non-WWE or WCW tag teams from the 1990s. Saturn had two partners from the Top 90 of the WrestleMania Era in Chris Benoit and Raven to work with in his title-winning scenarios, but he had just 25 combined days as champion to show for it. He was quite talented; one of the wrestlers who, if coming of age in the Brand Extension days of WWE, might well have padded his resume with more gold. He narrowly missed that window.

#196: Bryan Clark
2-time WCW Tag Team Champion

Clark is the first name on the list that might prompt a "Who?" He was a wrestler that was given a couple of horrible personas to portray in the gimmick-heavy mid-1990s, first as Adam Bomb in WWE and later as Wrath in WCW. Are there five guys from that era who were saddled with two lousier gimmicks than nuclear fallout man and a knockoff of a Mortal Kombat character? Only Kane (Isaac Yankem, fake Diesel) and Fred Ottman (Tugboat, Shockmaster) had it worse. Once he got to be just Bryan Clark, he had some success, teaming with Brian Adams (Crush) to form the two-time WCW Tag Team Championship-winning duo, KroniK. Their two reigns lasted just a combined 50 days, but that was par for the course in that era for both WWE and WCW. Clark was a guy that made the most of an opportunity during a period when WCW was actually giving a lot of chances to fresher talents.

#195: The Patriot
2-time WCW Tag Team Champion

In the late summer to late autumn of 1994, the primary feud over the WCW Tag Team Championships was Stars and Stripes vs. Pretty Wonderful. Paul Orndorff was the big star of the four, flanked by three notable mid-card acts from the mid-1990s in Mr. Wonderful's partner, Paul Roma (of Four Horsemen infamy) and the flag-waving babyface act consisting of The Patriot and Marcus Alexander (later "Buff") Bagwell. The duos traded the Tag Titles back and forth, with Stars and Stripes winning the feud with a victory at the 29th Clash of the Champions before becoming the first WCW Tag Championship victim of Harlem Heat. Del Wilkes had a gimmick built for the 1980s, but the masked American did his very best to outlast his expiration date, holding the Tag straps for 50 days and later making a splash against Bret Hart's anti-American persona in 1997.

#194: Xavier Woods
2-time WWE Tag Team Champion

Passion goes a long way in the pro wrestling business. It takes passion for a wrestler to overcome lousy gimmicks and still succeed; it takes the passion of the fans that get behind certain acts for wrestlers to get over; passion might quietly be the word that best describes the industry as a whole. Xavier Woods undeniably has passion. His zest for life helped bring The New Day into existence; the group was his idea and became one of the most entertaining gimmicks of the decade, thus far. As of Summerslam 2015, a pair of Tag Team Championships was the fruit of Xavier's labor.

#193: Mark Jindrak
2-time WCW Tag Team Champion

With two reigns as WCW Tag Team Champion alongside Sean O'Haire that were only two days longer than Bryan Clark's, Mark Jindrak checks in as another on the list of stars that might make you go "Who?" Young and shredded, Jindrak was high on potential and fairly low on talent, once seemingly a top prospect when he came into WWE after WCW folded, but never panning out despite several reasonably strong pushes. History tends to best appreciate the people who had less and accomplished more; Jindrak was a guy who had more and accomplished less. I award him just two points...and may God have mercy on his soul.

#192: The Mamalukes
2-time WCW Tag Team Champions

Clocking in with 60 combined days as the WCW Tag Team Champions, Big Vito and Johnny the Bull are the next on the "Who?" list. For those that do know who they are and are not Italian / do not know Italian people, "Mamaluke" is a slang term for a bum, often used in a joking manner amongst family and friends. There you go...you learn something new every day, capeesh? Did Vito prefer a bum or a cross dresser? You gotta love tag team names that make you consult an online dictionary; I'm guessing that there are some people that used one to look up "KroniK."

#191: Rico
2-time WWE Tag Team Champion

The smart wrestling fan contingency has a penchant for making some strange choices for the performers that they get behind. Zack Ryder was a recent case. While an unquestionably good athlete, some smarks were outraged when WWE ended Ryder's push. In all fairness to WWE, Ryder was given more than he had any right to get out of a narrow personality, a decent catchphrase, and a high vertical leap. A decade prior, similar support was thrown the way of Rico Constantino, blessed with comparable athleticism as Ryder and doomed by a similarly limited gimmick (plus he was already in his 40s when he broke in). He beat Ric Flair on TV once and huge things were supposedly on the horizon. Little ever came of him, though like Ryder he was enjoyable and won a few titles because of it.

#190: Bam Bam Bigelow
2-time WCW Tag Team Champion

In *The WrestleMania Era*, the Second Tier (#31-#60) was full of wrestlers who excelled in some of the five statistical categories yet were held back by others. Bigelow's primary weakness was his title record. Despite being generally regarded as one of (if not the) greatest super heavyweight wrestlers ever, he managed just 70 days as WCW Tag Team Champion as a member of The Jersey Triad (with DDP and Kanyon); that's all that shapes his mainstream (WWE and WCW) championship resume. His overall body of work – the quality of his matches and his WrestleMania main-event, particularly – was quite impressive, but it never translated to titles. There is a distinguished group in modern lore that one could argue "didn't need any titles." Is Bigelow on that list? I'm not so sure that he is, however great he may have been.

#189: David Otunga
2-time WWE Tag Team Champion

Do you remember in *Independence Day* when Jeff Goldblum's father teased him for going to M.I.T. so that he could become a TV repairman? The implication was clear: intelligence is a gift not to be wasted. For that matter, when it comes to wrestling, neither is a great physique. David Otunga, a former two-time WWE Tag Team Champion as part of the third best faction of this decade, The Nexus (#1 and #1A are The S.H.I.E.L.D. and The Authority; #2 is The Wyatts), is ironically blessed with both intelligence and physique and yet he seemingly wastes both. I admire a Harvard Law grad that chases his pro wrestling dream – I'm a doctor who wrote a book and is approaching a thousand columns about pro wrestling, after all – but if you're going to postpone the use of your mind to chase something your body affords you the chance to achieve, then be great at it!

(Tie) #188: "Dr. Death" Steve Williams
2-time WCW Tag Team Champion

In the last LOP column series-turned book that I wrote, *Starrcade vs. WrestleMania: A Prelude to the Monday Night Wars*, I was fortunate enough to write about certain wrestlers that I had never really had the chance to write about before; like Steve Williams, for instance. The man whose name caused Stone Cold to become Steve Austin was a beast of a talent back in the day. He competed as a member of the Varsity Club in the NWA, winning the Tag Team Championships for the first time in 1989. He later won the titles for a second and final time with Terry Gordy. There are some wrestlers whose title resumes make them out to be better than they were, but there are also some wrestlers whose title resumes do not reflect just how good they were; Otunga is in the former category, while Dr. Death falls into the latter.

(Tie) #188: "Mr. Wonderful" Paul Orndorff
2-time WCW Tag Team Champion

The same could be said of "Mr. Wonderful." Though undeniably one of the 90 elite wrestlers of the WrestleMania Era, Paul Orndorff was an infrequent champion. A brief period wrestling alongside Paul Roma as "Pretty Wonderful" in the early 1990s earned him two Tag Team Championship runs in WCW, but golden awards were not amongst the many things that he accomplished as a WWE star in opposition to Hulk Hogan and Roddy Piper at the height of his career in the late 1980s. A few breaks here and there and Orndorff could have easily joined his Hall of Fame peers in a higher position. Let it be made clear that he was amongst the greatest of his generation and that his lackluster spot on the Title list is the weakest point on his resume.

#186: Scotty 2 Hotty
2-time WWE Tag Team Champion

Scotty begins the wave of wrestlers who held the Tag Team Championships for a combined 100 days or longer. For Mr. 2 Hotty, it was 104 days to be exact (10 more days than Dr. Death). Like Williams, Scotty's two reigns were spaced out by a few years. Both his title-winning duos came with members of the Too Cool faction. The first in 2000 was with Grandmaster Sexay (who missed the cut due to the mere 27 day length of their reign). There wasn't a team that better fit the early 2000s; from their names to their dance to their look, they just scream of "Attitude Era." Scotty won the titles again with Rikishi in 2004, briefly recapturing the magic from 2000. W-O-R-M!

#185: Ted DiBiase, Jr.
2-time WWE Tag Team Champion

We live in a wrestling era in which there are far too many people that fail to stand out. In the Attitude Era, a guy like Scotty 2 Hotty was not oozing with charisma, but he did the Worm and danced like a fool and it got over big. Ted Dibiase was as bland as his wrestling trunks, never did anything to separate himself, and surely will be a forgotten wrestler for his time. Will anyone remember when he captured the Tag Team Championships twice with Cody Rhodes, who is a wonderful modern example of doing anything possible to get noticed? Dibiase is not Braden Walker (Who?) or anything, but he is in a class of turn-of-the-decade mid-carders who just didn't seem to want it that badly.

#184: Samu
1-time WWE Tag Team Champion

The Samoan Wrestling Dynasty is getting as much publicity now as it ever has before with the rise of Roman Reigns to the top of WWE. They're inductions into the Hall of Fame are plentiful (Rikishi, Yokozuna, and The Wild Samoans all in the last decade) and seemingly far from finished, Reigns is poised to become one of the next great stars, and The Rock is the biggest name in the history of the industry. It's safe to say that they've done more than alright. A forgotten member of their family is former Samoan SWAT Team member and Headshrinker, Samu, with whom Rikishi (as Fatu) won the WWE Tag Team Championships in the mid-1990s. They held the titles four months – the longest reign for a two year stretch between mid-1993 and mid-1995.

#183: Rosey
1-time WWE Tag Team Champion

It really was a statistical coincidence that Rosey, yet another member of the Samoan Wrestling Dynasty, wound up one spot ahead of Samu. A one-time Tag Team titleholder himself, Rosey combined with Hurricane to form the amusing superhero-type combo that carried the Tag Team division as champs for nearly 5 months. Of course, Rosey was not a full-fledged superhero. He was a S.H.I.T – a superhero in training. That has to be the preeminent acronym in pro wrestling's modern history, right? Wouldn't you like to be a fly on the creative team wall when someone comes up with stuff like that? Even the flies would roll their eyes. Who comes up with such S.H.I.T.?

#182: The Basham Brothers
2-time WWE Tag Team Champions

In thus far covering members of the greatest families and factions in wrestling lore, I am now curious to know what you'd say was the weakest faction. JBL's Cabinet has to be right up there, even if they are not at the absolute bottom of the barrel (where the likes of the Corre, the JOB Squad, and X-Factor can be found). Orlando Jordan is one of my least favorite wrestlers ever and the Bashams, while reasonably talented, never exactly lit the world on fire (they had a forgettable image consultant too). I remember a great LOP columnist named Davey Boy hyping Doug as a potential star; that possibility probably died when he debuted with a ball and gag in his mouth while being whipped by a dominatrix on his way to the ring. JBL tried to rescue him and his "brother," but they never clicked with any sort of consistency (2 Tag Title runs aside).

(Tie) #181: Evan Bourne
1-time WWE Tag Team Champion

What does it say about the state of WWE when over half of the stars on the rise in NXT and the main roster can do the things that were unique to Evan Bourne just five years ago? The level of ability to pull off so-called "indy moves" is seemingly a common trait these days. Clearly, the type of performer that WWE looks for today is changing, at least in terms of basic recruiting. Bourne came about in the wrong era then, one could argue. During his run in WWE, he could not stay healthy, mostly working with much larger guys. When he was healthy, he was a thoroughly enjoyable act. His 146 day Tag Team Championship reign with Kofi Kingston as "Air Boom" produced a temporary tag team renaissance that allowed the division to shine on several PPVs in late 2011.

(Tie) #181: David Hart Smith
1-time WWE Tag Team Champion

With a Tag Team Championship reign of 146 days, as well, the son of the future Hall of Famer peaked at a similar time as Bourne. He was the member of the Hart Dynasty who had the least amount of potential, though he proved serviceable as a performer. "Just a big, good looking kid" was a description that I read someone use to portray him in those days. That he was, but finding much more to say about him than that is no easy task. As a huge fan of Bret Hart and British Bulldog, I can say that the night that the Hart Dynasty won the titles was memorable to me and, thus, Davey Boy's kid had at least one memorable moment.

#179: Roman Reigns
1-time WWE Tag Team Champion

Tag Team wrestling has been consistently maintaining a better position in WWE since autumn 2013. Before then, the division would have its renaissance periods, but sustainability was lacking. Furthering the idea that The S.H.I.E.L.D. was one of the best things to have happened to WWE in a long time is the fact that it was the 148 day Tag Team Championship run by Roman Reigns and Seth Rollins that began the creative team's renewed sense of focus on the perennially underutilized wrestling genre. Reigns came of age during that time, quietly emerging by 2013's end as a budding singles mega-star. It would seem safe to predict that, in just a few short years, Reigns is very likely to become one of the all-time great WrestleMania Era champions.

#178: Rick Martel
1-time WWE Tag Team Champion

Before he became "The Model," Rick Martel joined up with Tito Santana to form Strike Force. With 5 months as WWE Tag Team Champions, the duo joined the ranks of the elite teams of the first golden era of WWE tag team wrestling in the WrestleMania Era. The division was stacked; whichever team reached the top achieved its status for good reason while many noteworthy squads failed to do the same. Strike Force is helped by its historically relevant break-up. Of the WWE Tag Team titleholders to unamicably part ways when Hulkamania was running wild, was there a more memorable one than Martel and Santana pre-HBK and Marty at the Barber Shop? Not in my book...

#177: The Soul Patrol
1-time WWE Tag Team Champions

There are all sorts of reasons to celebrate a championship win in sport or sports entertainment, but I think that younger fans may struggle to grasp the gravity of Rocky

Johnson and Tony Atlas becoming the first black Tag Team Champions in WWE history. The climate today may not necessarily reflect utopia in race relations (far from it), but I think it is important to remember how far we've come. Thirty years ago, it was a very open discussion amongst sporting executives that black men were not smart enough to quarterback football teams or run the point on basketball teams. In wrestling, the narrative read as "they" cannot be counted on to draw as champions. That's really not that long ago, folks. The Soul Patrol broke down a barrier with their 5 month title reign and the world has been better for it.

#176: Brian Pillman
1-time WCW Tag Team Champion

People can be called "pioneers" for various reasons. For some, it's becoming the first of your ethnicity to accomplish a goal; for others, the revolutionary contribution is more intangible. Take Brian Pillman as an example of the latter group; he was innovative for pushing the envelope with his character and blurring the lines between the performer and the man playing the TV persona. That resonates with a lot of people who appreciate the modern "reality" era where such a feat has become commonplace. Pillman was incredibly versatile; had he lived through the Attitude Era, he could have been a Swiss army knife for WWE, utilized for purposes across multiple divisions, racking up many titles in the process. Alas, his one championship was won with Steve Austin as the Hollywood Blondes.

#175: Rene Dupree
2-time WWE Tag Team Champion

A theme from the past that remains prevalent in both sports and sports entertainment is the notion that a certain amount of maturity is required to handle the spoils that come from being a professional athlete or entertainer. Though it was long since disproved that black people are not cerebral enough to steer a team's proverbial ship, it is still hotly debated that youth and success don't mix. Is Rene Dupree a good example of that adage in wrestling? He had all the potential in the world, but he debuted before his 20th birthday and won the first of his two Tag Team Championships before he had celebrated half a year on the flagship roster in the industry; he fell out of favor and was gone before he could ever rent a car. The French Tickler has endured in the minds of those that saw it and heard Tazz commentate it ("I'm a French Man, I'm a French Guy"), but Dupree is an overall distant memory.

#174: Steve McMichael
1-time WCW United States Champion

Accomplished former football stars have certainly made their mark on pro wrestling lore. Once upon a time, stars from the gridiron were having success in the squared circle with heavy frequency. Ron Simmons, Lex Luger, The Rock, and JBL are just a few that made the transition successfully. "Mongo" McMichael was another and he holds the distinction of being the wrestler who takes us out of the discussion of the greatest champions who made their marks only as Tag titleholders and moves us into the list of grapplers whose lone "golden" contribution was as leader of a mid-card singles division. McMichael was not particularly noteworthy otherwise, though his less-than-one-month reign as United States Champion did coincide with his time as a member of the legendary Four Horsemen. Was he the weakest member of any version of the famed stable? Or was Paul Roma. You decide...

#173: D'Lo Brown
1-time WWE Intercontinental Champion

The Monday Night War featured quite a few noteworthy factions, amongst them the Nation of Domination, whose most underrated member was D'Lo Brown. I wonder, in a parallel universe, could Brown have had X-Pac's career? Their career peaks were both in 1998, when Brown's Nation was feuding with Pac's Degeneration X. For various reasons, their relevancy ended two years later. Had Brown gotten the break in the mid-90s that X-Pac did, could it have been D'Lo wrestling Bret for the WWE title on Raw instead? Sean Waltman greatly benefited from his friends becoming some of the most influential wrestlers of the 90s too. Afforded the same chances via his clique, couldn't Brown have wound up a third tier star on the greatest ever list? I truly think so. He was a talented guy who parlayed his abilities into becoming the first ever Eurocontinental Champion (holding the European and IC titles simultaneously).

(Tie) #172: Albert
1-time WWE Intercontinental Champion

Matt Bloom, currently known as Jason Albert and formerly just Albert (among many other monikers), was a former football player, as well. In another era, he could have had a similar career as Vader. He was strong and agile as elite linemen tend to be, but the breaks never came in the USA for the A-Train. Whereas McMichael had a name but wasn't particularly talented, Albert was pretty damn talented but didn't have the same caliber of name. Albert still beats him on this list with 2 days longer as IC Champion than Mongo was as US Champion. He was probably a decade too late to make the biggest impact that he could have on-screen, but hopefully his work behind the scenes with NXT as a trainer translate to vicarious impact down the road.

(Tie) #172: Luke Harper
1-time WWE Intercontinental Champion

Of all the members of the 2012/2013 WWE rookie class that have ascended to modern era heights, perhaps the most intriguing career to watch will be Luke Harper's. Someday, he is going to break free from Bray Wyatt for good. How that happens may dictate his future success. He already proved that a brief period away from his "Family" member can yield championship gold of the Intercontinental variety. If his split from Bray in a longer-term capacity is a launching pad to the next phase of his career, the talented big man could become his generation's Kane – a multi-faceted, highly talented "big man" who develops creative Teflon, capable of having blunderous booking ideas bounced off of him without much damage done to Harper himself.

#170: Marc Mero
1-time WWE Intercontinental Champion

With a day longer reign as IC Champion than Albert, Marc Mero quietly sneaks into his inauspicious place in pro wrestling's championship history. When you rank, file, and present your findings, you see a spike in initial interest as people gravitate toward the basis of the concept; and, with a list as large as this one, you then see a dip in interest as the less relevant names begin to add up. Every list that I compile finds Mero occupying a similar spot as this one – right in the heart of the monotony. Yet, there is enjoyment to be found in the humdrum, as it gives us a chance to reminisce about the underrated athlete that was the former Johnny B. Badd, Marc Mero. He gave us Sable, so thank you, Wild Man.

#169: Rhyno
1-time WCW United States Champion

I enjoy studying psychological nuance. For instance, I like asking questions such as "How does a fan become a mark for a particular wrestler?" In other words, what is it about certain wrestlers to whom we develop a liking. Why do I mark for Rhyno? Why do I feel like if I was building a fantasy stable and I needed an enforcer, I'd definitely consider him, thinking that he would do his job and be fine being overshadowed as a personality by his stablemates? The answer? A video game. The former US Champ popped up as a Hardcore Title challenger on Nintendo Gamecube's WrestleMania X-8 and the "Chad Matthews" created character had to beat him. He gave me a heck of a match; "I" kicked out of the Gore and came back to pin him. And, hence, I mark for Rhyno. Who do you mark for?

#168: One Man Gang
1-time WCW United States Champion

For 33 days, One Man Gang was US Champion during a time in WCW history when the wrestling world's second banana was bringing in by-that-point jabronis – cast offs from WWE's 1st business boom (which had ended). I mark for Akeem in WWE; if there's any opposite term for mark in pro wrestling vernacular, then that's what I am for One Man Gang in WCW. Steve Austin was fired, but One Man Gang was hired? All due respect to the man, but he was the type that, if you had an inkling to check out what WCW was doing during the early Monday Night War and you saw him, he'd make you quickly flip back to WWE. He represented a failure to see where the business was going and a philosophy that WCW seemed to have for a bit, in which they acted as though living in the past would spark upward mobility in the present and for the future. If you're talking Hulk Hogan, then that made sense to a degree. If you're talking One Man Gang, then it most assuredly did not.

#167: Mr. Kennedy
1-time WWE United States Champion

Some might say that the use of the term "jabroni" above would aptly apply to this man, Mr. Kennedy. It seems hard to believe that, for about 6-9 months from late 2006 to mid-2007, the Green Bay Plunger hailed from the top of WWE's "next big star" ladder. He won the US title in the summer of 2006, feuded with Undertaker, headlined the Royal Rumble, and won Money in the Bank at WrestleMania. Then, he face-planted. I cannot think of a wrestler in the last decade (or longer) that seemed poised for so much and ultimately accomplished so little. He talked a big game, but never seemed to back it up with results. Perhaps his six week US Championship reign was a bad omen. For the next three years after he lost it, the average possession of the belt was 6 months.

#166: Kensuke Sasaki
1-time WCW United States Champion

Kensuke Sasaki might be the leader of the "Who?" list to fans of exclusively American wrestling. He quietly hit the American scene in WCW back in 1995, winning the US Championship from Sting at a New Japan Pro Wrestling event. New Japan, where Sasaki made his name, had a working agreement in the early-to-mid 90s with WCW. Starrcade '95 was the culmination of their joint promoting and was the site of Kensuke's loss of the US title to One Man Gang. Up until recently, we'd seen a large drop off in Japanese stars coming to the top USA-based promotions. Do we have Kenzo Suzuki's lousy run in the mid-2000s to thank for that? Was he so bad that he wiped out the pathway that Sasaki, Great Muta, Ultimo Dragon, Jushin Liger, and the like built in the 90s? Did I just create an excuse to heap some criticism on my least favorite wrestler pre-Great Khali? I think I did...

(Tie) #165: Bobby Lashley
1-time WWE United States Champion

Lashley gives Kennedy a run for his money as the best modern example of someone who seemingly was headed for 5 years or more as a WWE headliner before flaming out. The difference was that Lashley left WWE prior to falling so far from grace that he couldn't even execute a simple move without screwing up so badly that a top WWE star wanted him fired immediately. Had Lashley returned from injury in the spring of 2008, after having already won the US title, become the face of the new ECW brand, headlined WrestleMania, and had a breakout WWE title match against John Cena, he likely would have become a huge star and earned a chapter in <i>The WrestleMania Era.</i> Instead, he became a huge "What if?" He reportedly asked for his release because of racism; he may not have had a thick enough skin for pro wrestling, either.

(Tie) #165: Finlay
1-time WWE United States Champion

Tied with Lashley's 49 day reign as US Champion in WWE was Finlay, the Irishman who loved to fight and seemingly had far too solid a mid-card run in the mid-to-late 2000s (plus a respectable WCW run in the mid-1990s) to check in with just a lone major title to his name. Alas, here he sits. I'd take ten Finlays over one Kennedy or Lashley. All the potential in the world is useless if never realized. Finlay never had a ton of upside, but brought a unique style to America that allowed him to easily stand out when he wrestled. European wrestlers are thriving in the current era, thanks in part to the efforts of Finlay and men like him (Tom Billington, aka the Dynamite Kid, and William Regal, for example).

#163: Stan Hansen
1-time WCW United States Champion

Technically, Hansen held the US Championship for as long as the next guy held the IC Championship, so a tie is in order. However, the Intercontinental Title is WWE's brainchild. Call it a tiebreaker earned via victory in the Monday Night War, if you will. Anyhow, Hansen is a true legend in the wrestling business. In the 1970s, he was one of the biggest stars in the industry. His WrestleMania Era contribution was a lone 50 day reign as US Champ in 1990 born of a feud with Lex Luger, but his overall track record is definitely that of a Hall of Famer. It would shock me if he was not inducted in the next ten years.

#162: Ahmed Johnson
1-time WWE Intercontinental Champion

I feel as though we are constantly waiting for a transcendent black star in pro wrestling whose Samoan mom isn't part of a wrestling dynasty that confuses her son's African American-ness. I once asked my column readers who are black, "Do you think of The Rock as black?" Over half said, "No." In <i>The WrestleMania Era</i>, the premise of which was to statistically verify pro wrestling greatness, not one generally-thought-to-be black star cracked the top 30 (though Rock obviously ranked extremely high). Booker T was the closest. Amongst the many that seemed poised to become the dominant black star that could compete with the uppermost echelon of all-time greats was Ahmed Johnson. He had presence and power to spare, but that was about it. He won the IC title and held it for 50 days, but just never quite connected. WWE says that as much as a quarter of its audience is black, so surely someday that transcendent black star will emerge...

#161: Ezekiel Jackson
1-time WWE Intercontinental Champion

The transcendent black star surely never manifested in the form of Ezekiel Jackson. Again, I swear it was another statistical coincidence that Johnson and Jackson were back-to-back on this list. Big Zeke held the IC title for exactly one day longer than the Plunger from Pearl River, though his reign was not nearly as memorable. Johnson was catching on fast in his rookie year when he captured WWE's 2nd most prestigious title from the long-reigning Goldust in 1996. Jackson was gaining slight momentum in 2011 as a member of the clunky Nexus spinoff, The Corre, but he turned face when the faction flamed out and flopped as bad as his former stable. The IC title, back then, was vacillating between the 3rd and 4th most prestigious title, anyway. Unlike with Johnson, there was never any inkling that Zeke might be a breakout star.

#160: Chyna
1-time WWE Intercontinental Champion

Though Trish Stratus was the only female to earn a Top 90 ranking in my book, receiving a lower third tier spot, the most transcendent woman in wrestling lore is Chyna. Stratus had an overall skill set and a work ethic that put her in a class with her male counterparts. In fact, at her best, Stratus was better than many of the guys. However, she was never the star that Chyna was; no female ever has been. Chyna was incredibly unique and her two month reign as Intercontinental Champion during the most competitive period in sports entertainment history reflects that fact. She's the only woman to win a major championship. There will be another Trish Stratus assuredly, but there will never be another Chyna. The 9th Wonder of the World she was, indeed.

#159: "Hacksaw" Jim Duggan
1-time WCW United States Champion

Every title reign carries with it a certain context. That Jim Duggan's 100 day reign as US Champion in WCW came at the expense of Steve Austin has made it somewhat infamous. Duggan, like mentioned earlier with One Man Gang, was a WWE guy that had already hit his career crescendo and his star was fading fast. After losing the US belt to Hacksaw, Austin's career went into a tailspin and he was gone from the company within a year. There remained Duggan, who had never headlined a PPV and who had never been in a particularly noteworthy angle in his career, but Austin was let go. In a way, the Duggan-Austin dichotomy was a microcosm of the WWE-WCW rivalry. WCW said, "let us have your aging also-ran" and WWE said, "thanks, we'll take your 'mechanic' and turn him into the biggest star ever."

#158: Ryback
1-time WWE Intercontinental Champion

Ryback's 112 day reign as Intercontinental Champion in WWE may prove as forgettable as Duggan's US Title reign in WCW twenty years prior, what with "The Big Guy" being injured for a considerable stretch of it, but the context is what should separate them. It took Ryback five years to make it to the WWE main roster and a gruesome injury took him out of commission before he could ever capitalize on his position. When he came back two years later, he got over an old school gimmick in a hurry, got knocked way down the hierarchy after achieving considerable success, and battled back yet again to eventually win the Intercontinental Title, which may yet prove a career achievement, no matter if the unfortunate injury bug bit him at the wrong time once more.

#157: The Harris Brothers
3-time WCW Tag Team Champions

Another WCW flaw was how frequently they passed around championships. In 2000, especially, titles became props and lost much of their long-established value. Was it still prestigious to hold the gold and does it still show up in the record books that gold was held? Absolutely. Yet, again, context is key. The Harris Brothers held the WCW Tag Team Titles for less than six weeks total...over three reigns. That speaks to incoherent booking rather than staunch competition within the division. If there is a flaw in the title formula, it is that it rewards a championship won no matter how long it was held. The problem with devaluing a title reign because of its length is that length does not contextualize the meaning. Andre the Giant won the WWE Championship and held it for merely a few minutes; it doesn't change the fact that he was WWE Champion or that it means something.

#156: Shawn Stasiak
3-time WCW Tag Team Champion

Shawn Stasiak's tag team with Chuck Palumbo, "The Perfect Event," is another example of rapid fire title changes padding the stats of a wrestler not otherwise anywhere close to his peers, historically. In fact, if the Harris Brothers were among the top 5 least memorable wrestlers on this entire list, then certainly Stasiak might be too. I know that I, personally, best remember Stasiak for the backstage segments at Summerslam 2001 that saw him ineptly attempt to take out The Rock on behalf of the WCW/ECW Alliance. The 3-time WCW Tag Champ did have the pedigree for greatness (his dad was former WWWF Champion, Stan "The Man" Stasiak), but he was one of the second generation stars who never panned out. To his credit, once his wrestling career ended, he became a successful Doctor of Chiropractic in Texas.

#155: Heath Slater and Justin Gabriel
3-time WWE Tag Team Champions

Quick trivia question: can you name more than one duo in the modern era that won Tag Team Championships as members of two different factions? Other than Justin Gabriel and Heath Slater, I cannot recall another team to accomplish that feat. They were 3-time champions, once as members of The Nexus and then twice more as members of The Corre. None of the three reigns were memorable and assuredly these two will someday join Stasiak and the Harris Bros. on the list of least memorable names to win WWE or WCW titles. Gabriel did, though, have a wicked 450 Splash, which for a short time was presented as WWE's most devastating move.

#154: Chavo Guerrero
2-time WWE Tag Team Champion and 1-time WCW Tag Team Champion

This is how I like to think of Chavo Guerrero's mainstream pro wrestling career: he was a poor man's Owen Hart. He was a good enough character to stay consistently relevant for a decade and he was such a good wrestler that he could step up to the plate whenever WCW or WWE asked him to make a more significant than usual contribution. Matt Hardy makes for another apt comparison; Chavo was not as talented as his pseudo-brother Eddie (actually his uncle but separated by just 3 years) and his most famous work came either as Eddie's partner or his rival, so he tends to be overshadowed by that association. It was as if Latino Heat left T-Rex-sized imprints wherever he went and Chavo's raptor feet always stepped inside of them. Nevertheless, he accomplished a lot. He won the Tag Team Championships three-times and, had the third WWE brand not existed in 2008, he easily could have won the IC or US titles as a member of Edge's "La Familia" instead of the ECW title and been a few spots higher on the list.

#153: Paul Roma
3-time WCW Tag Team Champion

Have you decided on the all-time weakest member of the Horsemen between Roma and McMichael yet? Based on overall career accomplishment, Pretty Paul would get the nod over Mongo, but I'm quite confident that a compelling case could be made for Roma as the lowest on the totem pole. A handful of wrestlers per generation are gifted cushy spots and leave you wondering "Why?" Roma certainly fits that category. It did not take long for the Horsemen to give him the boot, though he did earn a Tag Team Title run with Arn Anderson. The bulk of Roma's 126 days as champion, though, came alongside Paul Orndorff.

#152: Billy Kidman
2-time WCW Tag Team Champion and 1-time WWE Tag Team Champion

Though being married to Torrie Wilson was undoubtedly the top byproduct of Billy Kidman's wrestling career, his WCW and WWE achievements are nothing to scoff at. His 132 combined days as a Tag Team Champion underscore his knack for finding a niche in either company. Popularizing the Shooting Star Press may have been the key to his success. Certainly in WWE, it seemed to be the basis for pushes, often putting him at the head of the class of high-flyers even though he was not nearly as high-flying as some of his cruiserweight peers. A move like that was always good for popping the crowd, so Kidman's finisher gave him a leg-up; his matches were not predicated on several flashy maneuvers, but one particularly stunning one. None of his title runs were particularly noteworthy, however.

#151: The Hurricane
2-time WWE Tag Team Champion

The post-TLC Era in WWE was a time in which memorable Tag Team Championship runs were hard to come by. The Smackdown Six combined their efforts in the fall of 2002 to make the Smackdown brand's golden duo straps quite prestigious, but beyond that, it was difficult to distinguish between a plethora of reigns that – even when unusually long – were never comparable to what was seen from 1999-2001 or in late 2002. The Hurricane's two runs as champion, first with Kane and then with Rosey, came in the midst of that lackluster period. It begs the question: from 2003 to the present, has there been a truly all-time great caliber Tag Team Title reign, combining quantity with quality of character and in-ring performance?

#150: Tyson Kidd
2-time WWE Tag Team Champion

Some wrestlers would have been perfect for the talent trading in the days of the big two promotions (WWE and WCW) and the cult favorite third (ECW); mark Tyson Kidd down amongst those who would have thrived back then. The last graduate of the famed Hart Dungeon has found success (and good health) hard to come by in his WWE career. He has managed to maintain his momentum once. In 2010, as a member of the Hart Dynasty, he held the Tag Team Championships for nearly 5 months. Then, he fell down the hierarchy until being randomly thrown into a Money in the Bank Ladder match. Unfortunately, he promptly got hurt and was out for a year. He was unable to get anything going again until 2014, but his very enjoyable and increasingly popular partnership with Cesaro was derailed by a neck injury.

Whenever he catches a proverbial break, his body literally breaks.

(Tie) #149: Pierre
3-time WWE Tag Team Champion

And

(Tie) #149: The Spirit Squad
1-time WWE Tag Team Champions

The Quebecers and the Spirit Squad each held the Tag Team Championships for exactly 216 days, the former over three reigns and the latter over seven consecutive months. Was one team more memorable than the other? It would be easy to give the nod to the Spirit Squad as wrestling history has had just the one male cheerleader conglomerate, but were they not just a more modern take on the classic industry trope of plucking a stereotype out of the easily teased-by-Americans hat? The Quebecers came from an era in which the go-to heel gimmick was someone not from the USA. That the Spirit Squad is from a slightly different class of the same tactic makes the teams a more interesting comparison. I would venture to say that the 'Squad was more unique, but that their time atop the tag division was less memorable; after all, even though Pierre and Jacques last defended the titles in double the number of decades as that of their counterparts, I can more readily recall one of their championship bouts over the cheerleaders' with ease.

#147: Don Kernodle
2-time NWA Tag Team Champion

Earlier on the list, a joke was made about a series of mostly dying-days-of-WCW wrestlers that made you go, "Who?"

Almost assuredly, Don Kernodle needs to be added, but not because he was a jabroni. Instead, it would be due to the fact that he is such an unknown commodity to such a vast part of the modern wrestling audience. When I wrote the column-turned-book, *Starrcade vs. WrestleMania*, I was stunned by the number of readers who told me that they had never watched a Magnum TA match. Let's assume that sample size is indicative of the broader fanbase. If so many have never watched Magnum wrestle, then have they even heard of the less-heralded Kernodle? Bearing in mind how important the tag scene was to the National Wrestling Alliance via Jim Crockett Promotions, Kernodle's multiple title reigns with Hall of Famers Bob Orton, Jr. and Sgt. Slaughter and sure-fire future Hall of Famer Ivan Koloff as partners should help explain his significance as a prominent mid-card act in the mid-80s.

The reign with Sarge didn't count because it came before the WM Era

#146: Brutus Beefcake
1-time WWE Tag Team Champion

The 7 ½ month Tag Team Title reign ranks as the highest honor in the career of Brutus Beefcake sans for his *Starrcade '94* main-event and his headlining match at *WrestleMania IX*. Only one of those three accolades is untainted by his friendship with industry titan, Hulk Hogan. It is rather amusing how one's associations can either help or hurt how people perceive you. Scottie Pippen, they say, never won anything without Michael Jordan. Though the reverse is also true, no one ever says that MJ never won anything without Scottie, do they? Rather than celebrate Brutus for his run with wrestling's "Dream Team" of Beefcake and Greg Valentine, Brunei is generally regarded as a wrestler who road Hulk's coattails to unfair advantages throughout his career. In his case, it's completely fair to say that Beefcake achieved nearly everything he did in wrestling because of Hogan. Something tells me he doesn't care. Do you ever wonder why we do?

#145: Lance Cade and Trevor Murdoch
3-time WWE Tag Team Champions

Reigning for four days longer over three times as many title runs as Beefcake were Cade and Murdoch, an enjoyable duo that always came across as old school and who could have used that old school thing called a tag team name back when only a few teams had one. For 230 days, they were the champs, highlighted by a series of matches with the Hardy Boys. It was in those matches that I felt they had earned the right to be highlighted by a team name. They were really good. Cade was well-respected by all-time greats, HBK and Y2J. Murdoch was a unique throwback to eras gone by with a body fit for a different time and promotion. Apparently, they were once known as "TNT." I cannot fathom why WWE decided against using that; it would have poked fun at the network that hosted their defeated competition (Ted Turner and WCW). Considering that jabroni duos who never accomplished squat earned team names, I vote we emblazon Cade and Murdoch as TNT from here on, rewriting history in the process.

#144: Charlie Haas
3-time WWE Tag Team Champion

One team that did not deserve a name was Charlie Haas and Rico, but that is by no means a knock on Haas. Blessed with rare chemistry in his partnership with previous Tag Championship cohort, Shelton Benjamin, Haas was involved in what was quite possibly the best tag team of the century. Originally known as Team Angle, Haas and Benjamin later boldly proclaimed themselves "The World's Greatest Tag Team." Boasting such confidence in your team name raises the stakes and demands a certain level of excellence. It's like calling yourself "God's Gift to Women"; you had better back up the claim or risk ruining your reputation. Haas and Benjamin truly were great, though, and they repeatedly excelled whenever given the opportunity. In fact, as was argued in *The WrestleMania Era*, they were the last great tag team in WWE.

#143: The Midnight Express
2-time NWA Tag Team Champions

After reading *Starrcade vs. WrestleMania*, a similar number of modern fans who had never watched Magnum TA wrestle commented on their limited exposure to the Midnight Express. To an enthusiast like me who grew up watching the NWA, it saddens me when people are not that familiar with the Jim Cornette-led group that included Bobby Eaton alongside both Dennis Condrey and Stan Lane. Fans today, who care about the quality of the performance as much as ever, would have adored Midnight's ability in between the ropes. They were awesome. Alas, this is a list of championship accolades. They held the NWA World Tag Titles for 244 days combined. They join Bam Bam Bigelow as the lowest ranked wrestlers who had dedicated chapters in the Second Tier of *The WrestleMania Era*, proving that while it is an important feat to achieve belts, championships are but one statistical category for shaping a definitive all-time list. The Midnight Express was far better than their limited golden trophy case suggests.

#142: The Usos
2-time WWE Tag Team Champions

If there is a tag team on the current roster that is seemingly poised to become the next historically great duo in WWE lore, then it is Jimmy and Jey Uso. The twin sons of Hall of Famer, Rikishi, have worked very hard to achieve their position as the featured team in a somewhat revitalized division. They debuted all the way back in 2010 and it took them four years to win the titles. Nowadays, that rarely happens. If a team is any good, they get hotshotted to the belts, have their brief stay as kings of the division, and then either split up or make way for the next flavor of the quarter year. The Usos slowly climbed the ladder to success one rung at a time, getting pushed aside in favor of thrown-together squads like Team Hell No and vanishing for stretches when WWE creative went through a period of forgetting about the tag scene, but right from the start of 2014 they caught fire. Their 202 day reign after they finally captured the Tag Team Championships was the 2nd longest of the decade. Not only that, theirs was easily the most critically acclaimed in the ring in ten years.

#141: Adrian Adonis and Dick Murdoch
1-time WWE Tag Team Champions

This is a good time to offer another reminder that only reigns from the WrestleMania Era (Starrcade '83 to the present) were considered for this list

Dick Murdoch and Adrian Adonis reigned supreme atop the WWE Tag Team division as champions for nine months. Their 279 day run was the sixth longest in WWE history. Murdoch is a relative unknown to modern fans. He was considered old school by the time the WrestleMania Era began. Perhaps most famous for his team in the 70s with Dusty Rhodes, Murdoch was a renowned tag wrestler who also had a successful partnership with Junkyard Dog in Mid-South Wrestling (despite being heavily accused of being a vehement racist). His WWE stint with Adonis – best known for his work as the effeminate "Adorable" character that came to blows with Roddy Piper at *WrestleMania III* – was the icing on the cake of a successful career. They won the Tag Team Championships from The Soul Patrol and dropped them nearly a year later to the U.S. Express. Once they split, Adonis changed gimmicks and became even more famous.

#140: Butch Reed
1-time WCW Tag Team Champion

One of the worst kept secrets in pro wrestling lore was the identities of the masked 281 day Tag Team Championship-reigning duo, Doom, in WCW. Ron Simmons and his partner, Butch Reed, were clearly under those masks and they had been on television as themselves not long before they suddenly showed up with their faces covered. The wrestling world does not churn out massively sculpted black guys all that often, so they were obviously Doom as much as Hulk Hogan was obviously Mr. America. Make no mistake, however; Doom was no joke in the ring. During their time together, they faced all and sundry – a Who's Who of WCW stalwarts from the early 1990s. They even feuded with The Four Horsemen. Domination was their game and they played it quite well. Of course, Theodore R. "Teddy" Long was their noteworthy manager. Doom was the longest reigning Tag Team Champions in WCW history, including the NWA roots dating back to the mid-1970s.

#139: The Dynamite Kid
1-time WWE Tag Team Champion

The British Bulldog (singular) was perhaps the greatest European wrestler in mainstream pro wrestling history. The British Bulldogs (plural) was perhaps the greatest tag team of all-time. With the third longest Tag Team Title reign of the WrestleMania Era, the Bulldogs were nearly as Iconic as Demolition, but an injury to their well-respected and innovative front man, The Dynamite Kid, prevented them from maintaining their spot atop of the WWE Tag world. If you ever get bored someday, look up Dynamite Kid vs. Macho Man on YouTube or the WWE Network. You'll note the date is 1986, but you'll marvel at the fact that, with better production value, it could just as easily have taken place in 2016. Don't confuse that as

Dynamite keeping up with Macho. In the ring, he was nearly as far ahead of his time as Randy Savage.

#138: Terry Funk
1-time WCW United States Champion and 1-time WWE Tag Team Champion

In *The WrestleMania Era*, a wrestler who made a significant contribution between Nov. 1983 and the present was not stripped of his golden accomplishments from before the original Starrcade, allowing men like Terry Funk, Harley Race, and Bob Backlund to excel in their championship statistics due to achievements in the 1970s and very early 1980s. This slightly tweaked analysis not including those pre-11/83 stats places Funk and Race in similar positions, far, far from where anyone would generally regard them amongst their championship peers. Funk was, of course, an NWA World Heavyweight Champion. The Hall of Famer is one of the greatest of all-time. His WM Era contributions were few in number, but powerfully impactful. I would venture to state that we will not reach as influential a wrestler on the product that shaped much of the second boom period (late 90s) until we get to the Top 30-50.

#137: Raven
1-time WCW United States Champion and 1-time WCW Tag Team Champion

Raven, who held the US Championship for the same paltry number of days during the Monday Night War as Funk, was influential in his own right as quite possibly the most psychologically deep wrestling character ever to that point in mainstream industry lore. Much like the Funker, his 1 day US title run and short reign as Tag Team Champion tells little about his pioneering role in the business. Raven was an artist who just so happened to fall in love with wrestling; his canvas ended up being a 20'X20' squared circle and the television and PPV programs that broadcast matches upon it. He currently sits as the last man on my list of the 90 greatest wrestlers of the WrestleMania Era. Technically, the list could constantly be tweaked and his position vulnerable, but considering the objectively subjective nature of that book, I will always have a hard time recreating that list and leaving him off of it.

#136: Marty Jannetty
1-time WWE Intercontinental Champion and 1-time WWE Tag Team Champion

Though not nearly as influential as Funk or Raven, Marty Jannetty's contributions to pro wrestling lore are horribly underrated. When you take into account that his tag team partner in The Rockers became the greatest in-ring performer of all-time and that his association with him became the basis for twenty years and counting worth of evaluating other duos to determine "Who is the Jannetty?" (aka "Who ends up with the comparatively insignificant singles career?"), then it is no surprise. To set the record straight, Jannetty's work with Shawn Michaels was the evolutionary next step in athletic tag teams and tandem maneuvers. Though The Rockers never won the Tag Team Championships (officially anyway – Marty's title winning partnership was with the 1-2-3 Kid), their style set the bar arguably so high that the TLC Era duos had to put their bodies through hell using furniture to top it. So, it may be fair to judge teams on "Who's the HBK and who's the Marty," but never fail to recognize the mark Jannetty left on the business.

#135: Zack Ryder
1-time WWE United States Champion and 1-time WWE Tag Team Champion

No, The Woo Woo Kid has not had the definably historic impact that have his peers listed immediately above him, but ten years down the road he might very well be heavily regarded as one of the most undervalued pioneers of his time. The US Title is probably the highest he will ever climb on pro wrestling's hierarchy. Yet, the story of how he achieved that honor will be his legacy. Ryder was amongst the first WWE stars to utilize social media as a means of establishing a fan following. To most casual viewers of the TV product only, he was a ghost. However, he started becoming popular amongst diehard fans via his YouTube-hosted reality series, *The Z! True Long Island Story*. He made himself a sensation that caught on with vocal audience members, who started chants for him on shows that he was not even booked to appear on. Within a year, he earned the US Championship. Even The Rock's first match in nearly nine years was peppered with loud "We Want Ryder" chants. That means something.

#134: The Godfather
1-time WWE Intercontinental Champion and 1-time WWE Tag Team Champion

Proving that anything to deal with sexual innuendo could get over like Rover in the Attitude Era, Charles Wright became one of the iconic acts of the Monday Night War by portraying the wrestling pimp, The Godfather. Championship gold had completely eluded him before in his ten year WWE career, but as soon as he started drinking the pimp juice, he became a bonafide success story. Though he ranks as one of the worst twenty titleholders in the history of the famed Intercontinental belt by length of reign (just 43 days) and perhaps one of the top ten worst by popular perception (he was a comedy mid-card act), Godfather – like Ryder – remains an example of how hard work eventually pays off. He also won the Tag Team Championships with Bull Buchanan.

#133: Dean Malenko
1-time WCW United States Champion and 1-time WCW Tag Team Champion

A nearly three-month reign as United States Champion in WCW allowed Dean Malenko – one of Raven's fellow fringe wrestlers at the bottom of *The WrestleMania Era's* Third Tier – to push ahead of an all-time great like Funk, while joining the Funker and Raven on the list of wrestlers whose title stats do not necessarily reflect their achievements. There has been much talk in the preceding pages about pioneering and hard work. Well, nobody ever outworked Dean Malenko in between the ropes. He had only rivals. Was he a pioneer? Put it this way – if asked to name five wrestlers from the 1990s who would have been huge stars in the era we're being ushered into today, Malenko would be on it. Eddie Guerrero would be at the top of it, but Malenko might not trail anyone else. He was that good. Never before has in-ring excellence been as greatly appreciated as it is right now. The Man of 1,000 Holds would have thrived in this current climate.

#132: Harley Race
1-time NWA World Heavyweight Champion

The legendary Harley Race held the NWA World Championship for a single night of what I define as The WrestleMania Era: the very first night of it, in fact. *Starrcade '83: A Flair For The Gold* was built on Harley's title defense against The Nature Boy in a Steel Cage match. He dutifully dropped the strap that night to Ric Flair and the rest was history. The torch passing moment removed him from a significant role in the rest of the long and storied rivalry between NWA/WCW and WWE. If you factor in his entire championship resume, then Race actually ranks in the Top 10 all-time using the Title Formula. Subtract everything he did before bringing the NWA Title to Greensboro, North Carolina on November 24, 1983 and here he sits – a titan of the industry's history being reduced to a spot on par with wrestling's pimp and wrestling's Situation.

#131: Vince McMahon
1-time WWE Champion

I may be in the minority, but I have always been of the mindset that Vince McMahon holding the WWE Championship was a mistake. I will never question how important a character he was during the most financially successful period in wrestling history, but I do question the logic in putting the most prestigious title in pro wrestling lore on a guy who, in 1999 when he won the belt, was still just an announcer on-air for twenty prior years. He had not had any of the matches, yet, that ultimately came to endear him to some of the more critical parts of the fanbase. He was already north of fifty years old and he was a horribly awkward performer. Frankly, it just came across as greedy; not in the sense that he owned the company so he booked himself to win the title for a week, but greedy because WWE was clearly kings of the wrestling world again and Vince winning the WWE Championship struck as massively hubristic – like they could do anything and get away with it.

#130: Sgt. Slaughter
1-time WWE Champion

Sarge is in the same class as Race and Funk as former champions who won a lot of gold before the WrestleMania Era. Post-November '83, though, he did win the most significant pro wrestling championship in existence at the *1991 Royal Rumble*: the WWE Title. I rather miss the days when WWE was still mostly PG, but didn't hesitate to take significant chances. During the rather tame period of the early 1990s, Sgt. Slaughter came in and portrayed a character that embodied the fears surrounding the USA having gone to war with Iraq. It was that envelope-pushing storyline that earned Sarge the WWE Championship and the main-event of *WrestleMania VII*. Would WWE execute a similar story today? Probably not. It was not all that long ago that they reportedly scrapped the original plotline for The New Day stable due to concerns of how it would look to the media following the Ferguson, Missouri controversy of 2014. It would sadly seem that the days of a heel skyrocketing to the top of the sports entertainment business on the back of a national current event with social education potential have long since passed.

#129A: The Great Khali
1-time WWE World Heavyweight Champion

In a case of journalistic adherence to detail being trumped by sub-conscious subjective abhorrence, The Great Khali was originally left off the list by accident despite his status as a former two month-reigning WWE World Heavyweight Champion. The book was finished and the editing process complete for the writing portion of the project when my wrestling content editor caught the mistake. Faced with the decision to reorder the ranking or just toss Khali into the appropriate spot with an "A" next to his number, I chose the easy route. After all, I figure he owes me (I'm kidding); I can never get back the hours spent watching him in the WWE ring (I'm not kidding). Khali is quite possibly my least favorite wrestler ever. (Mini rant alert) You have to actually be an athlete to be a professional wrestler. Trees blowing in the wind were more mobile than Khali.

#129: Ron Garvin
1-time NWA World Heavyweight Champion

If Vince McMahon is the worst WWE Champion of all-time, then Ron Garvin is the worst NWA Champion of all-time. Rugged Ronnie was a mid-card act through and through and belonged as NWA Champion in 1987 as much as Brutus Beefcake would have belonged as WWE Champion. It was just ridiculous and, at least to this pro wrestling historian, completely and utterly without justification. Lex Luger never beat Ric Flair for the

World title, but Ron Garvin did. If you were a fan back in those days, too, then you probably threw up in your mouth a little bit being reminded of that time.

#128: Mark Henry
1-time WWE World Heavyweight Champion

Amongst the things that the brand split accomplished for professional wrestling was the continuation of the long-held tradition of there being more than one mainstream entity in the business. For so long, multiple rosters produced World Champions so that there was not a monopoly on World Championships. Even though WWE owned both Raw and Smackdown, the extension to two separately functioning rosters allowed a lot of guys that might never have achieved maximum success in their careers to be stamped with a World Title stamp of approval. Mark Henry would have assuredly been one of the casualties of the total monopoly that wrestling has since been reduced to following the brand split's dissolution. Without Smackdown, he never would have grown so considerably in the twilight years of his career. It was a near impossibility for so tenured a veteran to improve that much anyway; take out the second brand and it almost assuredly never happens for the World's Strongest Man.

#127: X-Pac
4-time WWE Tag Team Champion

X-Pac / Syxx / 123 Kid was an outstanding wrestler and a key figure in the famed 1990s wrestling scene and that is why he is one of the greatest 90 wrestlers of the WrestleMania Era. However, his title statistics are a classic example of one of the worst things about pro wrestling during its most celebrated period. You may note from above that he has 4 reigns as a Tag Team Champion in WWE to his name. Their combined length? 77 days! That's less than three weeks per title reign. The futility would have been rendered less pronounced had his technical participation in the Hall and Nash 231 WCW Tag Team Championship run been counted, but X-Pac never once defended the titles on PPV and his inclusion in the record book was pure shenanigans. To his credit, Pac is the biggest casualty of not giving any credit here to holding the European Championship. Not many wrestlers did much with that title, but he sure did. There just was not enough history or lineage to include it; if I did not include the NWA/WCW TV Title, then WWE's 5 year foray into having a "Champion of Europe" sure wasn't going to make the cut either.

#126: Crush
1-time WWE Tag Team Champion; 2-time WCW Tag Team Champion

A general browse of the statistics reveals that Crush holding the WWE Tag Team Championships as the third member of Demolition gave him the bulk of his 198 total days as a Tag Team titleholder throughout his career, which would mean that he ranks one spot ahead of our next entry. However, Crush debuted two months into Demolition's final Tag Title run. He gets credit for his part of that title run because he was actively involved in its defense, most notably in a 2/3 Falls match at *Summerslam '90* against the Hart Foundation. Crush later added 50 days as WCW Tag Champ to his resume as a member of Kronik. Always good to have the chance to make brief mention of him. May he and the rest of the wrestlers who died too early Rest in Peace.

#125: Rob Conway
3-time WWE Tag Team Champion

For nearly 100 days longer than X-Pac, Rob Conway reigned atop the WWE Tag Team division. As a sympathizer to the French Canadian La Resistance, Conway managed to achieve a respectable (albeit forgettable) run in the mid-2000s. He was a wrestler who I found difficult to get a read on. Most guys debut and you can see something in them – good or bad – almost immediately. Roman Reigns, for instance, was green as goose poop (Rated PG), but you could clearly see the presence and discern he was going to be a huge star. Kenzo Suzuki, on the other hand, within three-minutes of his first match, clearly had to have shown WWE talent scouts tape of a more talented wrestler that looked like him; he was awful. Conway, though, never gave much of an impression of any kind. I remember him as distinctly "OK" across the board, from his look to his in-ring ability to his communication skills.

#124: Hardcore Holly
3-time WWE Tag Team Champion

When you think of WWE Superstars who had 15 year careers, Bob Holly is not going to be one of the first to come to mind; he is unlikely to be in the first dozen or two that come to mind. Yet, from 1994-2009, Holly was a consistent mid-card presence. Major title glory came his way just three times, all Tag Team Championships with three different partners. Of his 218 total days as titleholder, 202 of them came with a young Cody Rhodes under his wing. It would, however, be fair to state that the nearly seven month reign came at one of the weakest periods in Tag Team Title history since there was a set for each brand and there was not enough depth or creative focus to sustain both divisions. His 15 day run with his "cousin" Crash might have been slightly more impressive just because it took place when teams like Rock 'n Sock, The New Age Outlaws, The Dudleys, The Hardys, and Edge and Christian were in the mix. The other reign took place for 1 day in 1995 with X-Pac.

#123: Sean O'Haire
3-time WCW Tag Team Champion

The 257 combined days that Sean O'Haire reigned as WCW Tag Team Champion is a misleading mark in the record books because most of them occurred when WCW technically still existed under the WWE umbrella but had none of its wrestlers or champions actively competing. Take nothing away from O'Haire – I thought he was one of the most intriguing prospects to transfer from WCW to WWE after Vince McMahon bought the competition in 2001 – but there had not been a WCW Tag Team Title reign of over 100 days since 1997 by the time that The Natural Born Thrillers (O'Haire and Chuck Palumbo) won the titles at the third to last WCW PPV ever; the tag straps were bandied about like the belts that a group of friends in a wrestling club would trade back and forth in elementary school. Nevertheless, the Thrillers defended the titles at both WCW PPVs before the promotion was bought out and they carried their lineage over to WWE during the InVasion.

#122: Joey Mercury
3-time WWE Tag Team Champion

In discussing the Hurricane earlier, I questioned whether or not there was a Tag Team Championship reign from the post-TLC era to present day that was truly memorable. I don't personally believe there to be many candidates who combined the quality of performance and character, but MNM would be on the short list. Mercury, Nitro, and Melina were the consummate team of their day. Like the World's Greatest Tag Team before them, they were the cream of a boring crop, but they were the types that could have easily been transported to a different, more plentifully talented tag team era and thrived. They had a lot of great matches, racked up 291 days as Tag Team titleholders, and did what so few have been able to do over the last decade or more in staying the most relevant team long after their various title reigns concluded.

#121: Manny Fernandez
2-time NWA Tag Team Champion

If you subtract the random pairings of main-eventers that WWE has used to temporarily and unsustainably boost the tag team scene over the second half of the WrestleMania Era, then is there a wrestler from the last 30+ years with two more historically relevant Tag Team Championship-winning partners than "The Raging Bull" Manny Fernandez? There is no question that Jim Crockett Promotions knew what the heck they were doing with tag team wrestling. One of Manny's partners, Dusty Rhodes, was booking the territory; he knew the value of the Tag Team Titles. When positioned correctly on the card, the Tag Team Champions can draw near equally to the World (singles) Champion. With teams like the Andersons, The Russians, The Midnight Express, The Rock 'n Roll Express, The Road Warriors, and the Fernandez pairings with Rhodes and Rick Rude, why wouldn't tag team wrestling be box office if pushed as comparatively important?

#120: Bart Gunn
3-time WWE Tag Team Champion

Billy Gunn is considered amongst the top tag team wrestlers of all-time with his total number of championship reigns. There was a sizeable spike in the audience during the Attitude Era in WWE, meaning that most people would likely assume the Bad Ass to have achieved most of his success with The New Age Outlaws. Lest we forget that Gunn got his name from his partnership with *Bart* as the Smokin' Gunns in the mid-1990s. Bart and Billy had 331 total days of Tag Team Championship glory over three separate reigns. Though he was Jannetty-ed after they split, Bart probably *should* be remembered as a solid hand and a key contributor during a period in which the WWE roster was smaller and weaker. He *will* in all likelihood be remembered as one of the least memorable wrestlers of his time and a leading candidate to modern fans for the "Who?" list.

#119: Primo
2-time WWE Tag Team Champion

With a nine month Tag Team Championship reign – the longest since 2008 – plus one other title run to his name, Primo is one of the most underrated champs of the modern era based on length of time wearing gold. Hidden behind a mask in a limiting gimmick (Los Matadores), you might have to forgive certain parts of the fanbase if they forgot he was still around. Tagging with his cousin has proven less fruitful than tagging with his brother, but that would make sense given that Carlito was the most talented of the Colon boys to ply his trade in WWE. Primo joins Bart Gunn on the list of higher ranking "Who?" wrestlers, but anyone who reigns atop a division for 280 days should be commended, especially when considering that it was during that reign that Primo and Carlito unified the Smackdown and Raw Tag Team Championships on the pre-show of *WrestleMania 25* – perhaps the best pre-show match (including Heat) ever and the one that might have been the most memorable for its significance.

#118: Test
1-time WWE Intercontinental Champion; 1-time WCW Tag Team Champion; 1-time WWE Tag Team Champion

Test earned his place on this list in the manner opposite of Primo. Whereas the latter was defined by one lengthy title reign, Test was defined by short bursts of championship glory...very short bursts. Test partnered with Booker T during the InVasion to win the WCW Tag Team Titles...for 13 days. He and Booker won the WWE Tag Team Titles a few months later...and held them 13 days. Just prior to the *2001 Survivor Series*, Test won the Intercontinental Championship and merged it with Edge's US Championship in a losing unification effort...13 days later. Such statistical anomalies happen so rarely that I will confidently state that there will never be another wrestler who holds three different titles for the exact same lengths of time again.

#117: Tajiri

1-time WCW United States Champion; 2-time WWE Tag Team Champion

A tiebreaker was necessitated by Tajiri and Test each holding a secondary WWE singles title for a day less than two weeks; and Tajiri's two Tag Team Championship reigns were far lengthier than Test's. I was there to see one of Tajiri's golden Tag Team days. *Judgment Day 2003* saw the Japanese Buzzsaw replace Chavo Guerrero as Eddie Guerrero's partner in a Ladder match against Team Angle. The Guerrero and Tajiri duo produced hilarious television. Tajiri was actually quite a versatile character for someone who rarely spoke. He could be funny, endearing himself to the audience as a babyface. He could play the serious heel leader of an evil faction. He could just be a scrappy mid-card talent in a more traditionally heroic role. To get a 5 year WWE career out of that? Makes him pretty underrated in my book.

#116: R-Truth

1-time WWE United States Champion; 1-time WWE Tag Team Champion

I have a harder time contextualizing the career of R-Truth than someone like Tajiri or Test. You always knew what you were getting with those guys. Test was the big, well-trained athlete who got it done in the ring but had limited charisma. Tajiri had a cool move set that could always be delivered in a 5-minute match. What does R-Truth consistently bring to the table? He has spent as much if not more of his WWE career as a hapless jabroni mid-carder who disappears for months at a time between meaningful appearances. Yet, he has had moments of brilliance that leave you astounded and wondering, "Where the heck did that just come from?" See the post-WrestleMania season of 2011. He went from dancing, rapping, gimmicky guy to main-eventing a PPV against John Cena in the blink of an eye, utilizing a persona that bordered on the insane – and did it incredibly well. So, yeah, he won a couple of titles, but 2011 will always beg the question: "Shouldn't he have accomplished a lot more in nearly a decade?"

#115: Umaga
2-time WWE Intercontinental Champion

Umaga should be used as the prototype for the modern "monster" heel. WWE had for so long used gigantic oafs to portray scary bad guys. As the fanbase became more demanding and less tolerant of horrible matches, they had to change it up a little bit. Enter the latest entry on this list from the Samoan Wrestling Dynasty: Umaga. The Samoan Bulldozer was a beast in between the ropes. He was agile enough to come flying off the top rope routinely and strong enough to execute power moves with relative ease. His huge backside added a weapon for him. You take someone like The Great Khali, who it bears repeating might be my least favorite wrestler of all-time, and put him against a top talent and he does look intimidating, but he's also borderline incompetent and once killed a guy pre-WWE. Umaga, a two-time IC Champion in WWE, was made to look ferocious, and then went out and made it look like he was demolishing heroes. He was a legit pro wrestler and not just a guy gifted a chance because of his size. Umaga paved the way for talents like Rusev.

#114: Rusev
1-time WWE United States Champion

Built like Umaga, the Bulgarian Brute has been an incredible addition to the WWE roster so far in his career. Like the previous entrant, Rusev does not have a physically marvelous look, but he is a physical marvel. Burly, fast, and technically sound, there's not really anything that Rusev can't do in a wrestling ring. He's basically an Eastern European version of Umaga. Blessed with a versatile personality that the Samoan Bulldozer never showcased, Rusev can achieve greater things and add many more championship accolades to his resume. As it stands, his 5 month reign as United States Champion culminating in a headlining match at *WrestleMania 31* has already pushed him far ahead of several noteworthy peers on the countdown of champions. With as international an audience as WWE has today, perhaps Rusev could become to this and future generations what Kane has been to so many recent eras: a multi-faceted character that can be used all over the card depending on where he's most needed.

#113: Orlando Jordan
1-time WWE United States Champion

Thanks to John "Bradshaw" Layfield's record-long WWE Championship run in 2004/2005, Orlando Jordan is ranked ahead of several Hall of Famers. I don't like to be too negative about even wrestlers that I don't particularly care for, but OJ had one of the worst title reigns I've ever seen. It was such a disproportionate display of length of the reign (nearly 6 months) to what was actually accomplished during the reign (virtually zilch) that I would genuinely be OK if it was discovered that he had bribed Vince McMahon to make him US Champion, creating enough negative publicity that WWE decided to expunge the OJ title reign from existence ala Reggie Bush's Heisman Trophy being nullified. They should put this guy's picture next to the word "jabroni" in the encyclopedia.

#112: Andre the Giant
1-time WWE Champion; 1-time WWE Tag Team Champion

If you could go drinking with any wrestler in history, would it really be anyone other than Andre the Giant? Wouldn't you just want to see whether or not all the stories were true? I think if I had a time machine, I'd bring ten bucks with me to around 1985; right when Hogan was making it big and usurping Andre's status as WWE's top draw, but still at the point where he felt like he had something to prove to The Giant when they went out for cocktails. I'd bring just ten dollars so that I wouldn't be so happy to be drinking for so comparatively cheap a price that I got tanked and missed my chance to count Andre's drinks. Could he really drink over 100 beers? What a legend, though. The modern tendency for newer fans to crap on Andre's matches needs to stop. He could barely walk during the early WrestleMania Era, but he still produced the biggest wrestling match ever. If you can't take a step back and celebrate that, then I don't know what to tell you.

#111: The Iron Sheik
1-time WWE Champion; 1-time WWE Tag Team Champion

So, let's say that time travel does exist and you get to make that trip to the mid-1980s to go drinking with Andre and Hogan. I don't know about you, but if Iron Sheik doesn't show up at some point in the night rambling and ranting, I travel back to the future disappointed. As for the Sheik's in-ring career, there were only five WWE Champions between 1980 and March 1990 and he was one of them. Cut from a similar cloth as Ivan Koloff in the 1970s, the anti-American antagonist took the title off of one legendary hero (Bob Backlund) only to drop it shortly thereafter to another (Hulk). The venerable "Real American" was established through his defeat of the dastardly Iranian and the rest is history. Sheik is perhaps the most underrated contributor to the early WrestleMania Era, with his incredible feud against Sgt. Slaughter immediately following his run against the Hulkster. His proceeding Tag Team Championship collaboration with fellow Hall of Famer, Nikolai Volkoff, continued to pour lighter fluid on the red hot patriotic sentiment of that period.

#110: Sylvain Grenier
4-time WWE Tag Team Champion

Recent WWE history has trended toward doing what so many diehard wrestling fans have always clamored for: let the best pro wrestlers in the world (who can talk and wrestle) get a chance to showcase their skills in the most recognizable promotion on the planet (WWE) regardless of how they look. The problem with Vince McMahon describing himself as being in the "entertainment" business is guys like Sylvain Grenier – the antithesis to the modern trend. Grenier looked like a male model. So, the fact that he through-a-garden-hose-level sucked didn't matter. He became a 4-time WWE Tag Team Champion and ranks ahead of Andre the Friekin' Giant as a WrestleMania Era titleholder. There are pros and cons when viewed both ways, but the greatest advantage to looking at WWE like the NBA instead of Hollywood is that looks don't matter in pro sports; it only matters how good you are. If you look good but you're no good, then you're out.

#109: Brian Kendrick
2-time WWE Tag Team Champion

The influence of the independent scene on modern day WWE would have greatly benefited Brian Kendrick a decade ago. Kendrick still had a more than respectable run in the first decade of the 21st century, peaking with his inclusion in a 5-man

WWE Championship match in 2008, but WWE had to go through a lot of Greniers before they finally decided to go after Kevin Owens-types. Formerly nicknamed Spanky, Brian Kendrick came of age during the run of dominance on display in WWE by the OVW Class of 2002. Given his cruiserweight look and style, he was demoted to the floundering tag team division. Once partnered with a similar wrestler, Paul London, he found his niche en route to one of the longest reigning WWE Tag Team Title runs ever (331 days). The London/Kendrick duo currently holds the record reign for the lineage of the current Tag Team gold, originally debuted on Smackdown in 2002. If you add in their brief, South African house show tour-sponsored 3 day run with the Raw belts, then they are actually the 9th longest reigning tandem in the entire history of tag team wrestling in WWE.

#108: The Road Warriors
2-time WWE Tag Team Champions; 1-time NWA Tag Team Champions

In terms of all-time great tag teams, everyone competes for second place behind The Road Warriors. With one year combined in their three mainstream Tag Team Championship reigns, they were not able to collect the amount of stats to be featured highly on this list, but combining all the categories that shape the term "greatness," they are the cream of the crop. You name the team: either of the Expresses, the Freebirds, the Bulldogs, the Hart Foundation, Demolition, the Hardys, the Dudleys, Edge and Christian; it doesn't matter. Hawk and Animal are almost above the tag team genre in pro wrestling, with all due respect to it. They belong in a conversation reserved for the World Heavyweight Champions, in terms of their impact and ability to captivate an audience. Call them The Legion of Doom or The Road Warriors; call them WWE Hall of Famers; call them the only team to win the NWA, AWA, and WWE Tag Team Championships. The bottom line is that if you ever saw their unique combination of hulking physiques complimented by intensely patterned face paint when they were in their prime, then you remember them in the same vein as you do Austin, Rock, Hogan, Flair, and the like.

#107: The Rock 'n Roll Express
4-time NWA Tag Team Champions

Whereas the Road Warriors transcended their era, The Rock 'n Roll Express were perfect fits for their time. They are one of those teams that achieved so much in the WrestleMania Era, but are virtually unknown to a great deal of the modern wrestling fanbase. I've been writing about wrestling for over a decade and there is a big difference in the group of writers that join me today across the vast worldwide web and the ones that were around when I began scratching my journalistic itch. Some of the best, most knowledgeable columnists know little to nothing about a team in the conversation for the greatest babyface tag team ever. With 400 days combined as NWA Tag Team Champions, Ricky Morton and Robert Gibson are more decorated than the Road Warriors and Midnight Express who, outside of Arn Anderson's Four Horsemen teams, were the primary historical rivals for Rock 'n Roll in the NWA of the early Mania Era. Yet, they get a lot less of the all-time hype. They are a team worthy of your educational energy. WWE Network was made, in part, so that you could emphasize that old tagline from WWE 24/7: **Play, Rewind, Relive.** You'll get a lesson in the basic craft of tag wrestling from Morton and Gibson.

#106: Jacques Rougeau
1-time WWE Intercontinental Champion; 3-time WWE Tag Team Champion

Jacques Rougeau holds the unique distinction of being one half of a historically celebrated tag team who earned the majority of his professional championship accolades in a far less historically celebrated tag team. He and Raymond formed the

Fabulous Rougeaus. In an era when house shows meant more to the business than they have in twenty years, the Rougeaus were very well received as an opponent of all the late 1980s greats in WWE. Yet, they never won the Tag Team Championships, meaning that Rougeau might be better remembered for winning the Tag Team Titles three times in what many would call an inferior team in an inferior time period. After Raymond moved on, Jacques was repackaged as The Mountie in a gimmick annoying enough as a heel to earn a 2 day reign as Intercontinental Champion. Then, another wrestler showed up wearing the same outfit and the Quebecers were born. Thus, Pierre makes this list many pages ago and Raymond is sadly just a footnote.

#105: The Fabulous Freebirds
1-time WCW United States Champion (Hayes); 2-time NWA/WCW Tag Team Champions

The erratic history of the Tag Team Championships in mainstream pro wrestling history is reflected in the fact that so many of the recent entries are all-time great tag teams. Next up is The Fabulous Freebirds: Michael "PS" Hayes, Terry "Bam Bam" Gordy, Buddy "Jack" Roberts, and (sometimes) Jimmy "Jam" Garvin. As alluded to in *The WrestleMania Era*, The Four *Horsemen* surely deserve to be the reason that factions are also called *stables*, but the team that laid the groundwork for what pro wrestling groups could be was the Freebirds. The "Freebird Rule" (allowing all members of a faction to defend Tag Team gold) has given them a lasting legacy that most fans can identify, but they were also the first wrestlers to enter the arena to rock music and redefined the bond formed between stablemates. What The S.H.I.E.L.D. has been celebrated for – unity, brotherhood, and definiteness of purpose - is what the Freebirds believed to their core. They could have accomplished more, but they never wanted to split up. The consummate "package deal," they stuck together even when it was potentially detrimental to their individual careers (especially

Hayes, who was eventually a United States Champion in WCW while still repping the Freebirds). True legends. Look them up, too.

#104: Kanyon

1-time WCW United States Champion; 2-time WCW Tag Team Champion; 1-time WWE Tag Team Champion

While you're going back through NWA/WCW history to take in some footage from these tag teams, take a detailed look at Chris Kanyon too. When researching *The WrestleMania Era*, a number of WCW talents whose skills I had forgotten about over the years stood out to me as being extremely underrated, particularly as it pertained to the creativity used in their move sets and counter wrestling. Perhaps the most underrated was Kanyon's 3-time Tag Team Championship-winning partner, Diamond Dallas Page. Yet, Kanyon was amongst that group too. Though kind of like Test in that he had a lot of brief title reigns that positively skewed the perception of his relatively weak overall career (at least on the historical ranking scale), Kanyon was a lot of fun to watch in between those ropes. Once nicknamed "The Innovator of Offense," he could work with anyone of any style. Akin to Cesaro today, Kanyon was a wrestler whose matches you didn't want to miss. His longest title reign was a 48 day run with the United States Championship during the InVasion.

#103: Bill DeMott

2-time WCW United States Champion; 1-time WCW Tag Team Champion

We still have plenty of jabronis to get through, but the latest is Bill DeMott. First impressions matter. My initial exposure to DeMott was when he got mauled by Bill Goldberg. He came out to the ring as Hugh Morris. Yuk yuk. The next memory of him was when he portrayed General Hugh G.

Rection. Pat Macrotch and Jack Meoff were taken I guess. Even when I was sophomoric, sophomoric humor was hit or miss with me. DeMott always missed. Nevertheless, the "Rection" persona won three major titles in the autumn of 2000. He won the United States Championship twice for a combined total of two months and held the WCW Tag Team Championships, as well. General Hugh G. Rection having any sort of prominent place in professional wrestling's history books is embarrassing. I've written an epic book and a couple of smaller books on this pro wrestling genre of sport/entertainment. Don't you know how much I love it that I'm writing about General Hugh G. Rection right now and attempting to be serious? Dying days of WCW to us wrestling historians is what the Lockout Season is to NBA historians.

#102: Val Venis

2-time WWE Intercontinental Champion; 1-time WWE Tag Team Champions

Now, here's a guy whose sophomoric character was a big hit with me. If you were somewhere between middle school and college when Val Venis was climaxing in the Attitude Era and you tell me that you never cut a Big Valbowski promo, I'm going to assume you're a liar. WWE owned WCW when it came to the brand of television that made Venis famous. The wrestling porn star gimmick was portrayed well enough to where I can sit here right now in my mid-thirties and remember the images from his Titan Tron visage – the hot dog and the drill (LOL). It didn't hurt that Sean Morley was a helluva talent who could cut those hilarious pre-match promos and then get it done as well anyone in the ring. His 83 days combined as Intercontinental Champion were well-deserved. From 1998 to 2000, he was a legitimate second-tier star in WWE during the most competitive stretch in the history of the business. That says something. The Tag Team Title run with Lance Storm when he converted to his real name as an Eric Bischoff lackey was well after his peak.

#101: Ken Shamrock

1-time WWE Intercontinental Champion; 1-time WWE Tag Team
Champion

Only two men held the Intercontinental Championship
for longer than 100 days during the Attitude Era. One was The
Rock and the other perhaps his second greatest Intercontinental
Title rival, Ken Shamrock. Coming from UFC back in the day
when WWE was the far superior draw and the better place to
earn a living, Shamrock brought something unique to the table
with his credentials alone. That was a time characterized by
finding ways to stand out. He did not need a flashy persona or
catchphrase or gimmick to separate himself from his peers
amidst the most competitive stretch in WWE lore. Shamrock
being Shamrock was quite enough. From his run in 1997 as a
borderline psychopathic babyface to his heel turn and stint as a
member of the Corporation, "The World's Most Dangerous
Man" was a gamer. In addition to his IC title, he also had a
short-lived WWE Tag Team Championship reign with Big
Bossman.

#100: Dick Slater

1-time NWA United States Champion; 1-time WCW Tag Team
Champion

15 years before Shamrock held the IC Title for 125 days
and later held the Tag Team Titles for 42 days, Dick Slater was
United States Champion for 129 days and later held the Tag
Team Championships for 57 days. However, Slater is a strange
case on a list in the WrestleMania Era. He was one of those
wrestling nomads held over from the territory days.
Establishing his name in the southeast when regional fanbases
were the norm, he excelled in all of the promotions based from
the Carolinas down to Florida and out to the Midwest. When he
went north during the early part of the first boom period, he

could not repeat his southern successes. Nevertheless, he won the US Title right after the first Starrcade when that strap was white hot coming off the Roddy Piper vs. Greg Valentine feud. Unlike many of his peers, though, he never became the kind of star that had staying power in one of the major companies. Though undeniably a historically relevant talent, Slater was decidedly better off before wrestling hit the mainstream.

#99: Curtis Axel
1-time WWE Intercontinental Champion; 1-time WWE Tag Team Champion

There are a few wrestlers in positions similar to this one that should probably thank their lucky stars that they are ranked anywhere near this highly. Curtis Axel, to his credit, is a very hard worker and a solid hand in the ring, but many a fan would happily toss him onto the Jabroni squad and forget about him. It might surprise those enthusiasts to know that Axel is actually the 5th longest single reigning Intercontinental Champion of this decade. With a three month run as WWE Tag Team Champion during his time in the unsuccessful continuation/reboot of The Nexus, Mr. Perfect's kid has had a pretty respectable career. Let's be honest, though; when you're a second or third generation star, you cannot escape comparisons to your father. Some do whatever they can to break free of the shadow (see the Rhodes boys), some make people think of their fathers as "so and so's dad" (see Rock and Orton), and others just don't have anything close to what their fathers had (see Brian Lawler and Ted Dibiase, Jr.). Axel vacillates between the first and third categories.

#98: Drew McIntyre
1-time WWE Intercontinental Champion; 1-time WWE Tag Team Champion

The third longest single reigning Intercontinental Champion of the decade is Drew McIntyre. In 2010, it looked like this decade was going to be dominated by European stars hell bent on taking what Davey Boy Smith started in the 1990s to the highest possible level. WWE had expanded its television reach to unprecedented heights, helping to offset the drop in domestic TV viewership. McIntyre was joined by Sheamus and Wade Barrett and did not seem out of place when mentioned in a conversation with them as the top Euro talents. Vince McMahon even publicly called him a "Future World Champion." His 5 month reign as IC Champion certainly seemed the start of something big. Then, it turned out that the Euro Class of 2009/2010 could not upend the OVW Class of 2002 (no different than any other class to that point). Years later, McIntyre is gone and the others have been joined by a plethora of other international talents trying to join the 1st NXT Class as the future of the business. Hindsight is fascinating, isn't it?

#97: Kerry Von Erich
1-time NWA World Heavyweight Champion; 1-time WWE Intercontinental Champion

Back in the early 1980s, there were a lot of people that thought Kerry Von Erich would be one of the biggest stars in the industry. From a more territorial-perspective which did not yet embrace the massive shift to national brands, you could argue that Von Erich was one of the biggest stars of the 1980s. I maintained in *The WrestleMania Era* that if you began as a wrestling fan in the 60s and 70s, you might be bound to overvalue that period, making claims like "there were many WrestleManias before the first WrestleMania." And, with all due respect, you sound silly when you say that. It's like comparing the 1950s NFL to the present time; there's no comparison. That Kerry Von Erich is a former NWA World Champion inflates his value. He was a huge territory star given a World Championship run that meant very little nationally. In an age of 300 day average title reigns, his was just 18 days. The decision to put the belt on him was made by a nationally expanding company stuck in the mindset of a failing system. No disrespect to Von Erich, of course, but we saw what he could do on a national scale when he flopped as Intercontinental Champion in WWE; the average IC Title reign from 1983-1990 was 253 days and Von Erich's was just 84 days.

#96: Jack Swagger
1-time WWE World Heavyweight Champion; 1-time WWE United States Champion

By now, it seems that I was in the minority of fans who immediately developed an attachment to Jack Swagger when he quickly ascended to the top of the ECW brand in 2008. I saw amateur singlet, grappling holds, and the All-American pedigree and thought of Kurt Angle – one of my all-time favorites. "Swagger will replace Angle," thought a younger me. My faith in young Jack seemed justified when he became World Heavyweight Champion eighteen months later and I thought he excelled as the cocky jock heel. Yet, with a title reign that lasted less than 90 days and merely an above average career since, it would again seem that I was one of the few that bought in. Barring a forgettable United States Championship run, Swagger has done little to separate himself from the pack in a loaded mid-card scene to break into the role of consistent main-event threat. He wound up being more Ken Shamrock than Kurt Angle, but wrestling will always need Jack Swagger-types.

#95: Buff Bagwell
6-time WCW Tag Team Champion

If you call Buff "Marcus Alexander Bagwell" in conversations, then you're dating yourself as a wrestling fan...and I high five you from afar. The more that time passes, the less I find myself chatting with fans that watched WCW. Bet you didn't expect to see this guy on the list this highly did you?

The ranking is facetious. He held the WCW Tag Team Championships six times for an average of 18 days. I need a stat guy to check on whether or not that is a record low average title reign for someone with at least six championship runs. It has to be. Bagwell was around from the early 1990s until WCW got bought out and never managed a major title reign of over 28 days. He adds another noteworthy distinction by being the only wrestler ever to have one of his championships shared on paper with his mother. His title-winning partnerships included The Patriot twice (as Stars and Stripes), Too Cold Scorpio, Scotty Riggs (as The American Males – creative huh?), Rick Steiner, and Shane Douglas.

#94: Paul London
3-time WWE Tag Team Champion

Seeing as we have already covered the record WWE Tag Team Championship reign of London and Kendrick, it seems appropriate to use London to create greater context for the era that we're watching. You see, he's really the perfect example of what fans perceived to be Vince McMahon's attitude toward the typical independent wrestler of the 2000s: small, too many flippy moves, and oblivious to the intricacies of sports entertainment. In fact, it could also be said that London personified what traditional-thinking executives thought that the diehard fans, loosely defined by the word "internet," wanted pro wrestling to be (even though it wasn't true). He did find some success as a multiple time Tag Team Champion with Kendrick and Billy Kidman, but London did himself in when he was caught laughing on camera during a (ridiculously over-the-top) segment on Raw involving the Chairman. It could not have better exemplified the perception of London-types vs. WWE brass.

#93: Jim Neidhart
2-time WWE Tag Team Champion

Though the Hart Foundation never held the WWE Tag Team Championships quite as long as London and Kendrick, they are the only team in the WrestleMania Era (WWE or WCW) to have two separate Tag Team Title reigns of 7 months or longer. Considering the outstanding quality of their matches when combined with that impressive statistic, there should be no questioning the Hart Foundation as one of the top 5-10 tag teams ever. Additionally, they outlasted most of their peers in WWE, which laser-focused on one team at a time as the faces of the division; among the duos that won multiple Tag Team Titles in the era of (generally) longer reigning champions, the Foundation were the only to separate their reigns by two years or longer. They earned top billing in 1987 and then again in 1990. Jim "The Anvil" Neidhart was obviously a big part of that. He was the tough guy that added an extra layer of legitimacy to the Pink and Black Attack in an era of giants.

#92: Rikishi
1-time WWE Intercontinental Champion; 3-time WWE Tag Team Champion

Just what was it about the Monday Night Wars that caused both WWE and WCW to switch championships around so frequently? During the first nine years of the WrestleMania Era, the Tag Team Championships in WWE changed hands on an average of every six months (nearly). Ditto for the Intercontinental Championship. In the next nine years, which encompassed the WWE Attitude Era, the Tag Team Titles changed hands almost every month and the Intercontinental Title just over every six weeks. If you account for the transition periods of a year or two that blended the end of Hulkamania into the WWE New Generation and blended the end of Attitude into the Brand Extension, then you see some lengthier title reigns remain the norm in the early 1990s before the dam broke and an improvement to a happier medium in the mid-2000s after the dam was partially rebuilt (10 week avg. IC title reigns since 2003, for example). Rikishi represents the craziness of title switching (14 day and 16 days reigns as IC and TT Champion respectively), the transition to the craziness (4 months as TT Champ), and the happier medium (11 weeks as TT Champ).

#91: Shane Douglas

1-time WWE Intercontinental Champion; 1-time WCW United States Champion; 2-time WCW Tag Team Champion

Perhaps the answer to the question posed at the beginning of the previous entry is that the promotions decided that they wanted to add a shock element to their proceedings. Shane Douglas was case in point. As the evil Dean in WWE circa 1995, he and Razor Ramon won the Intercontinental Championship on the same night, with The Bad Guy emerging as the three-month reigning titleholder. If they wanted Razor to hold the strap, why not just have him win it outright instead of two champs in one night? The reason was "surprise." Where do you think that old adage that "anything can happen in WWE came from?" It came from a consistent string of nights where an arguably better story was sacrificed in favor of forced unpredictability. Guys like Douglas benefited. He won the WCW Tag Team Titles with Ricky Steamboat before the championship change bonanza, but all the rest of his mainstream golden trophies came during a title change-heavy period. That does not mean he was not talented, no more than it means Rikishi or anyone else wasn't, but it does skew the rankings in their favor.

#90: Tully Blanchard

1-time NWA United States Champion; 2-time NWA Tag Team Champion; 1-time WWE Tag Team Champion

I find it far more impressive that someone like Tully Blanchard was able to put together his resume during an era in which title switching was kept at a premium. Thanks to his 130 days as United States Champion, he ranks ahead of the aforementioned by-products of a more pass-it-around happy age. With over four months as the reigning titleholder, it's possible to leave your mark on the industry. How any champion can be expected to help add or sustain viewers by holding a belt for just a couple of months (or especially less than a month) is beyond me. Of the quadruplet of titles that Blanchard won, three were held between 130 and 180 days. Thus, he left a considerably larger mark on the NWA in the late 1980s than most of his WrestleMania Era peers. Granted, it could be argued that Rikishi, despite being a Hall of Famer, never had the chops to accomplish what Tully did, but couldn't we argue that Shane Douglas – based on his work in ECW alone – absolutely had what it took to equal Blanchard's resume in a mainstream promotion? If WWE or WCW had focused four months worth of title attention on him instead of 3 weeks maximum, I believe the conversation about his career would be quite different.

#89: Konnan

1-time WCW United States Champion; 2-time WCW Tag Team Champion

Granted, all having a lengthy title reign does is give a guy a chance. He either makes the most of it or he doesn't. You might get mixed opinions as to whether or not Konnan made the best of his 5 month United States Championship reign. For my money, anyone who holds a title for 160 days and loses it to Ric Flair on the same famous PPV that gave birth to the New World Order has to be given the benefit of the doubt and termed a success. He parlayed his US Title run into a reasonably successful WCW career. Konnan was a member of the N.W.O. and was later a prominently featured roster member when popular hip hop artist, Master P, was regularly on WCW programming. He also formed a faction called the Filthy

Animals, winning the WCW Tag Team Championships twice with stablemates, Rey Mysterio and Billy Kidman. Like Douglas, though, Konnan was far more influential outside of mainstream pro wrestling (he was/is a huge star in Mexico).

#88: Big E
1-time WWE Intercontinental Champion; 2-time WWE Tag Team Champion

There's a popular conversation among modern wrestling historians about whether a championship makes a man or a man makes a championship. Using the previous entry as an example, Konnan's career profile has been boosted – call it "made" – by his run with the US Championship, the reputation of which was built – call it "made" – by the likes of Tully Blanchard. As with many things in life, that discussion probably focuses too heavily on black and white constructs. In the second half of 2015, it would have been difficult to argue against Big E's New Day faction *making* the Team Titles more important by virtue of their popularity heightening the tag division's place in the WWE hierarchy. On the other hand, I'd argue that Big E was originally *made* by his 167 day reign as Intercontinental Champion. Did he enhance the title's stature? No, the title's stature enhanced Big E; the IC Title gave him a platform to improve. So, does the title make the man? Does the man also make the title? Big E provides a good example that the answer to both questions is, "Yes."

#87: Bob Backlund
2-time WWE World Heavyweight Champion

Bob Backlund and Harley Race are very similar in modern pro wrestling lore. When the WrestleMania Era began in earnest during the build-up to the original Starrcade, Race was the reigning NWA Champion and Backlund the reigning WWE Champion. Both would lose their respective titles within a month of each other and quickly become relics of an era gone by. Their respective places in overall history were shaped before the WrestleMania Era began and have, thus, taken considerable backseats to the career retrospectives of the Hogans and Flairs of the wrestling world. The major difference between them is that Race *managed* the heel who won the World Championship from WCW's top babyface of the early-to-mid-1990s while Backlund *was* the heel who won the World Championship from WWE's top babyface of the early-to-mid-1990s; hence Bob's superior position on this list.

#86: Chuck Palumbo
2-time WWE Tag Team Champion; 4-time WCW Tag Team Champion

Quick: what's the first thing that comes to mind when you think of Chuck Palumbo? Is it the nearly ahead-of-its-time wedding to Billy Gunn that fizzled out before the "I do"? Or is it the 205 day reign as WCW Tag Team Champion with Mark Jindrak? Surely it's not the latter. Either way, I figured I would need to jolt you a little bit for you to engage in something written about Chuck Palumbo this far along on the list. He may seem out of place, but his title resume isn't. 381 days combined over six Tag Team Championship reigns is nothing to scoff at. Then again, he was clearly a product of his time. No way Palumbo racks up that kind of trophy case a decade before or after his peak. Also, recall that his 205 day Tag Title reign was misleading because most of it took place while WCW was caught in limbo between WWE's purchase and the Invasion storyline.

#85: The Nasty Boys
1-time WWE Tag Team Champions; 3-time WCW Tag Team Champions

Let's play a little game. You take a wrestler or a tag team from one era and trade him or them with a comparable wrestler or team from another era with an expectation of similar success. An easy example would be to switch John Cena and Hulk Hogan. A popular trade a few years ago was CM Punk and Steve Austin, but I'm no longer as sure of its efficacy. Do you have faith that Punk could excel in the most competitive period in wrestling history? Do you even have faith that Steve Austin could be as successful as the man who bucks the system when the system he's bucking is so different? Not always so easy, is it? Alright, who do you trade for the Nasty Boys? I'd pick the Dudleys. Similarly non-traditional body types by modern standards, both loud and obnoxious, and each surrounded by all-time great level duos against whom they were so unique. Plus, as you'll see in due course, their title resumes were very similar. The bulk of the Tag Team Championship success accumulated by Knobbs and Sags came from a 155 day reign in WWE from *WrestleMania VII* (over the Hart Foundation) to *Summerslam '91* (a loss to the Legion of Doom) and a 210 reign in WCW. Overall, they held Tag Team gold four times to become one of the most recognizable duos of the early 1990s.

#84: Arn Anderson
5-time NWA/WCW Tag Team Champion; 1-time WWE Tag Team Champion

If we continued the above game, how do you translate the perfect southern combination of technical skill, power, selling, and verbal ability into any of the periods that followed the NWA's early Starrcade Era? I'm not sure that Arn Anderson fits anywhere beyond the era in which he thrived. He was a combined six-time Tag Team Champion with three-and-a-half month average title reigns, making him quite possibly the most accomplished tag team wrestler of the first third of the WrestleMania Era. Some in the tag division were as good in the ring, but nobody was definitively better. When he got the chance to work singles, he excelled; he just never got the major gold to show for it. Nevertheless, he decidedly fit the southern pro wrestling model and was unquestionably an upper tier mid-carder (not a solo main-eventer, though legendary for what he did accomplish). Finding an adequate trade partner proves difficult. To pay him the respect that he deserves, it's best to simply call "The Enforcer" an incomparable talent and leave it at that, allowing his 614 days as a Tag Team Champion in WWE and NWA/WCW to speak for themselves.

#83: Demolition
3-time WWE Tag Team Champions

This is the entry that sees Tag Team Championship success reach its zenith in the WrestleMania Era. Demolition combined for 700 days over three reigns in WWE. Only The New Age Outlaws, The Steiner Brothers, Harlem Heat, and The Hart Foundation are anywhere close and they're all at least 180 days behind. If anyone ever again gets that close, it will be a major surprise. It begs the question to me as to how in the hell *Pro Wrestling Illustrated* only listed them 59th on their all-time list of tag teams back in 2003. As my own book attests, there's plenty of criterion that shapes a "greatest of" list, but surely one of them is the dominance shown over your peers as the champions of a division. What more could Demolition do to establish their dominance? During very important years historically, they ruled a Golden Age of WWE tag team wrestling as both babyfaces and heels. The only other duo to accomplish that feat pre-TLC was the Hart Foundation, who were never as feared as the antagonists and never celebrated as much as the protagonists.

#82: Carlito
1-time WWE Intercontinental Champion; 1-time WWE United States Champion; 1-time WWE Tag Team Champion

Now, we turn our attention to a group of accomplished singles mid-card champions, beginning with the man who spit in the faces of people who didn't want to be cool. Back in 2004, Carlito (Caribbean Cool) had the wrestling world at his finger tips. Just in his early twenties and the son of a future Hall of Famer, he seemed poised to be one of the industry's top stars when he defeated John Cena for the United States Title in his first televised match on Smackdown. On his first night on Monday Night Raw in 2005, he won the Intercontinental Championship from Shelton Benjamin. Yet, for whatever reason, he just never advanced. He became one of the rare individuals whose best night was his first night. Interrupting the eventual Golden Boy of WWE in the early part of the show and taking the US Championship in the main-event later on...can you name any night in his career that came even close to that? He stayed in WWE until the end of the decade, even winning the Tag Team Championships with his brother in a duo that also unified the Raw and Smackdown brand Tag Titles, but the Colons were an afterthought.

#81: Cesaro
1-time WWE United States Champion; 1-time WWE Tag Team Champion

I think that there is a quiet expectation amongst many sections of the WWE fanbase that believes Cesaro will rack up a lot of championships during his career, even amidst an increasingly competitive environment. He's just that good in the ring; he's of a caliber that Carlito could never have dreamt of achieving. The announcers like to talk him up as the "pound for pound strongest man in WWE." I'd add that he's also "pound for pound" one of the most versatile performers of the WrestleMania Era. He could wrestle a great match against Big Show, Sin Cara, and anyone in between. Despite the general consensus that he's one of the most underutilized talents in WWE over the last few years, he does have a United States Championship reign to his credit that ranks in the top 20 longest of all-time; his name on that list is sandwiched by Steve Austin, Shelton Benjamin, Sting, and Jimmy Snuka (each overall Top 90 guys). It remains to be seen if he'll ever win the big one, but he strikes me as the type that would be right at home racking up lengthy IC, US, or Tag Team Title runs for the next half decade.

#80: The British Bulldog
1-time WWE Intercontinental Champion; 2-time WWE Tag Team Champion

Could Cesaro become his generation's Davey Boy Smith, only without the Wembley Stadium heroics? That's a possibility, though British Bulldog was arguably the most successful European ever to wrestle in WWE (he ranks ahead of Andre statistically), giving the Euro influx of talent in the modern era an excellent historical pacesetter. Smith's championship success doesn't really tell the full story of his impact, as impressive as his resume may be with his two Tag Team Championship runs of a combined year and a half (10th and 13th longest reigns in WWE lore) and his monumental IC Title victory at Summerslam in London over Bret Hart in 1992. He headlined a lot of PPVs in the 1990s off the back of his Summer Classic success. He was a viable contender to the likes of Vader and Shawn Michaels at the peak of their powers, if that says anything about Smith's ability. So, to replicate his success, a European star would need to be one half of arguably the greatest tag team ever and be so popular that WWE would put him in the main event of the second biggest show of the year. It might be awhile.

#79: William Regal
2-time WWE Intercontinental Champion; 4-time WWE Tag Team Champion

Of course, many Europeans in the business today would probably settle for being their generation's William Regal; and that may well be the more realistic era-to-era comparison for Cesaro. The Swiss Superman possesses many of the same traits as Regal, who utilized his immense wrestling skill set to earn six major championships in his career. The Power of the Punch (brass knuckles) gave Regal his first Intercontinental Championship in early 2002. He won the title again nearly seven years later. In between his top singles runs were four reigns as Tag Team Champion (twice with Lance Storm and once each with Eugene and Tajiri). I will, personally, be disappointed if Cesaro becomes the Regal of the modern age considering that Regal is one of the greatest wrestlers of the WrestleMania Era who never actually got to showcase the full extent of his capabilities. If the three main ingredients to wrestling stardom are looks, wrestling acumen, and verbal ability, then wrestling fans like us generally want the latter two to be emphasized most. Regal was a maestro on the mic and a stalwart in the ring, but he was missing the appearance. Nevertheless, he accumulated over a year's worth of title reigns in his career.

#78: Wahoo McDaniel
2-time NWA United States Champion; 2-time NWA Tag Team Champion

One of the most enjoyable aspects of creating a long-form historical analysis is educating younger fans about talents like Wahoo McDaniel. Though a wrestling legend in the Southern to Midwestern United States in the 1970s and 1980s, McDaniel was quite an accomplished football player and popular personality in the New York market while playing for the Jets. A linebacker, his tackles would be followed by the PA announcer prompting the crowd with the question, "Tackle made by WHO?" to which they would respond "WAHOO!" He started wrestling to supplement his professional football income, which back in the 1960s was peanuts compared with today. One of the most successful men to ply his physical trade on both the gridiron and the 20'X20' canvas, Wahoo eventually retired from football to focus only on wrestling. The class of

1995 WCW Hall of Fame inductee proceeded to put together one of the most sparkling championship resumes of the Territory Era. The fact that just four of his overall 30(+) titles count toward his WrestleMania Era resume does not do his overall career justice. A veteran of the first four Starrcades, his golden contributions from Nov. 1983 onward include a shade over a month as Tag Team Champion and 174 days as United States Champion.

#77: Magnum TA
2-time NWA United States Champion

Younger wrestlers would kill to have the kind of momentum that Magnum TA built in the mid-1980s as the focal point babyface of the NWA United States Championship division. In legendary feuds with Tully Blanchard and Nikita Koloff, Magnum became one of the hottest commodities in the business before tragedy struck him down in a cruel twist of fate. We'd be discussing him a lot later if it were not for a rainy day and slick roads causing him to wrap his Porsche around a telephone pole. He never wrestled again after that accident, largely condemning him to the "What if?" category of wrestling lore. Magnum was en route to the World Championship, however. You can read more about the specifics in *Starrcade vs. WrestleMania: The Prelude to the Monday Night Wars*. For 302 days between 1985 and 1986, he reigned as US Champion, but he was the kind of game-changer that exemplified the adage "the man makes the title." Whenever he was involved, Magnum made the US Title seem as important as the NWA World Heavyweight Championship. Consider, for a moment, that the NWA Champion for the bulk of those years was Ric Flair; and, then, let the gravity of that compliment weigh on you.

#76: Dean Ambrose
1-time WWE United States Champion

Many discussions are had among pundits about the prestige of titles. My contribution to these conversations typically revolves around WWE's creative effort toward championships, which shapes fan perception of a title's importance. Earlier, I wrote about one of my least favorite wrestlers ever, Orlando Jordan, having a United States Championship reign that accomplished next to nothing. Now, I love Dean Ambrose, one of the biggest stars of the Reality Era, as much as the next fan; he's an incredibly gifted all-around performer destined for World Championship gold. Let's face it, though: there may not be a less accomplished US Title reign of considerable length ever in the WrestleMania Era. On paper, his 351 day reign is an incredible achievement. He is, in fact, the longest reigning US Champion in WWE history, the 3rd longest single reigning US Champion of the WrestleMania Era (NWA/WCW lineage included), and the 8th longest total reigning US Champion of the WrestleMania Era. However, Ambrose's reign embodies the 21st century booking tendency to seemingly forget that a title exists. He rarely defended the US Title. While holding any belt for a year looks good on your resume, I'll never remember it as having done anything for him (or vice versa). As good as he is and as great as he may become, he is one of the worst US Champions of all-time.

#75: Don Muraco
1-time WWE Intercontinental Champion

Allow me to make the case for why Don Muraco should have been included in the Top 90 in *The WrestleMania Era* instead of being the last wrestler cut from the first edition. The original Rock was the fourth man to capture the Intercontinental Championship in the title's history, but he is the man responsible for establishing the value of the title to the modern wrestling fan who began watching during the last 30 + years of WWE industry dominance. Commentators regularly remind that Pat Patterson was the first IC Champion, but the iconic image of Snuka splashing Muraco from the top of a 15 foot high steel cage is the "picture worth a thousand words" of Intercontinental Title lore. It is to the IC Title what Hogan slamming Andre is to WrestleMania: the original iconic moment of its glory. Muraco won that match by the way; the Superfly Splash from the cage was not the means to victory, but the response to defeat. It should be noted that, technically, just three months of Muraco's 385 days as IC Champion (the 3rd longest single reign of the WM Era) should have counted for this list. However, in a moment of subjective objectivism, I gave him credit for the whole reign. I have always felt that I slighted him in leaving him out of the Top 90 in my first book, so this is just my small way of acknowledging his legendary career. Muraco is the 75th greatest champion – the diamond entry – of the WrestleMania Era.

#74: Tito Santana

2-time WWE Intercontinental Champion; 1-time WWE Tag Team Champion

The man who took the Intercontinental Championship from Don Muraco and made his own case for being the one who initially defined what an IC titleholder should be was Tito Santana (who did make the cut for the overall Top 90 of all-time). With a pair of 200+ day reigns with the belt, the sensation from Mexico certainly made a name for himself. Add in his Tag Team Championship run as one half of Strike Force and he was one of the most decorated wrestlers of the original wrestling boom. Strange then, it is, that he is so infrequently mentioned in modern conversations about the top Latin stars of the WrestleMania Era. He had longer than a decade to leave his mark and he unquestionably left it, so why does he take such a backseat to his fellow Latinos? I don't think anyone could argue that he deserved a place ahead of Mysterio or Guerrero in the hierarchy, but surely he's right behind them as their forebear, neck and neck with Alberto Del Rio based on his impact alone and with Del Rio's uncle Mil Mascaras based on his overall golden trophy case in the world's most recognizable pro wrestling promotion.

#73: The Honky Tonk Man
1-time WWE Intercontinental Champion

Championships certainly aren't everything in pro wrestling, but the Intercontinental Championship was everything to Honky Tonk Man. His record 454 day reign was the sole reason for his consideration and ultimate inclusion in *The WrestleMania Era* Top 90 list. How can you ignore that, especially when he won the title from the man who had the match that launched the IC Title into the argument for being the world's second most important wrestling championship (though it would lose that argument to the NWA World Heavyweight Title and wind up being the world's third most important title)? It makes you forget that an Elvis impersonator has held the IC Title reign record for three decades. The bottom line is that there's not much more to the wrestler than that record, at least in regards to golden accolades, wins, or losses. That one and only title run defined the Honky Tonk Man.

#72: Santino
2-time WWE Intercontinental Champion; 1-time WWE United States Champion; 1-time WWE Tag Team Champion

The legacy of many of the preceding entries has long since been defined. I think it's going to be interesting to see what sort of mark on history will be reflected upon when discussing Santino Marella. For several years, an argument could be made that he was the most entertaining character on WWE TV. That is a comment that speaks volumes about what he accomplished, as is the fact that he cracks the Top 75 overall titleholders of the WrestleMania Era. Yet, just a few years removed from his injury-forced retirement from the ring, it is difficult to get a read on how history will remember him. His championship accolades, on the surface, seem to be a tip of the hat to the entertainment value that he added. He spent 329 days as either IC or US Champion (not bad at all) spread across his 2007 debut ("The Milan Miracle") to the early part of 2012 (when he arguably peaked in the WWE pecking order). We likely won't talk about him for his title reigns and will instead focus on how hard he made us laugh, but his golden trophy case should be remembered as a tangible expression of his worth.

#71: Mike "IRS" Rotunda
5-time WWE Tag Team Champion; 1-time NWA Tag Team Champion

Taking into account the WrestleMania Era only, Mike Rotunda is the third most successful tag team wrestler in WWE lore. And it would surprise me if that didn't surprise you. Even without recognizing his NWA Tag Team Championship reign back in the Varsity Club days, Rotunda was a massive success, first as one half of the duo that carried the WWE Tag Team Titles into *WrestleMania 1* and later as the other half of the team that dominated the tag division during the transitional period between the end of Hulkamania and the start of the New Generation. It was the latter pair that puts him in the Top 75, as Money, Inc. (with Million Dollar Man) earned Rotunda (as IRS) 411 days as champion over three reigns. I never much cared for their matches, but – looking back – that probably is a reflection of WWE's declining interest in the tag team scene. What once was an incredibly deep division felt the wrath of declining business, leaving a very top heavy division in its wake. The Steiner Brothers and Road Warriors joined Money, Inc. as the cream of the crop, but it was rare that you would see the creative deployment of their talents in a manner on par with their 1980s counterparts; if there was a predominant reason for it being a surprise that Rotunda is ranked here, that is surely it.

#70: "The Million Dollar Man" Ted DiBiase

1-time WWE Champion; 3-time WWE Tag Team Champion

On February 5, 1988, Ted DiBiase pulled off one of the greatest antagonistic moments in pro wrestling's entire history. Earl Hebner, foreshadowing in fascinating fashion a much more iconic instance of treachery, fast-counted Hulk Hogan's shoulders to the mat, causing the long-reigning WWE Champion to lose the title to Andre the Giant. Andre, who had tried to get the title off of Hogan for a year, quickly showed that he was more interested in money than he was in being champion of the world; he handed the belt to The Million Dollar Man, who had used his monetarily-driven influence to essentially buy the WWE Championship. It was ten times as incredible as it reads. However, the more time passes between that moment and present time, the more important it is for that title reign – no matter how brief – to be officially recognized in the WWE history books. Without it, the narrative on DiBiase's career doesn't change overall – he still has 411 combined days as a WWE Tag Team Champion in the final days of the first golden tag team era - but it is done a disservice. There aren't ten more memorable WWE Title wins in the WrestleMania Era; and none are more infamous.

#69: Dusty Rhodes

1-time NWA World Heavyweight Champion; 1-time NWA United States Champion; 1-time NWA Tag Team Champion

The birth of the WrestleMania Era predates the first WrestleMania by my estimation. The modern age of pro wrestling truly began when the nationalization of the industry led to the first supercard as we know it: *Starrcade '83*. The Dusty Rhodes-booked, Jim Crockett-promoted spectacular predated *WrestleMania 1* by a year and a half. Vince McMahon surely caught wind of Starrcade's 40,000 closed circuit viewers and thought to himself, "I can do that and do that a lot better." The Starrcade vs. WrestleMania dynamic is an essential cog in understanding the history behind the Monday Night Wars. The American Dream was a huge part of the early NWA-WWE rivalry, both on-screen and behind the scenes. His World Heavyweight Championship victory over Ric Flair during the '86 *Great American Bash* is the only of his three reigns taken into account for this historical ranking and, though his ensuing run lasted just two weeks, it – like Dibiase's in 1988 – was one of the most memorable in history. Dusty's rivalry with Ric Flair is iconic; winning the title in a Steel Cage match gave him the cathartic victory that he'd sought since 1984.

#68: The Dudley Boyz
9-time WWE Tag Team Champions; 1-time WCW Tag Team Champions

Unlike Rhodes and DiBiase, The Dudley Boyz had no single title victory that necessarily stood out above the others, but the sheer volume of their championship wins stands out considerably. Ten combined Tag Team Championship reigns is an amazing achievement. From the start of the second golden era of tag team wrestling until the division drifted back to mediocrity in the mid-2000s, it could be argued that the Dudleyz were *THE* tag team; the measuring stick duo to whom all others were compared. They reigned as Tag Team Champions every year from 2000 to 2004. They even main-evented a PPV against the Undertaker (horrible concept and match though it was). Critics will point to the fact that their combined number of days during their ten reigns was 328 (an average length of just a shade over a month), but that was a product of the times. No team was more important to the rise of tag team wrestling in the Attitude Era than they were. No other pairing whose sole contribution to this list is Tag Team Titles will be ranked ahead of the Dudleys. That says something.

#67: Matt Hardy

1-time WWE United States Champion; 7-time WWE Tag Team
Champion; 1-time WCW Tag Team Champion

Fitting, is it not, that one of the greatest rivals of the
Dudley Boyz ends up right after them on the countdown. Matt
Hardy reigned twice less than the grand total of ten times that
did the Dudleys, but his United States Championship run in 2008
boosted his profile slightly above theirs. Hardy's chase of the
US Title throughout 2007 until an untimely injury knocked him
out of action was one of the best mid-card storylines of the last
decade. MVP, of course, had a phenomenally long reign as
champ during that time, pushed even further by Hardy's
inability to compete for a few months. Hardy and MVP actually
added a Tag Team Title reign to Matt's trophy case, joining the
seven other duo Championships won with his brother, Jeff. In
all, Matt Hardy had 243 combined days as a Tag Team
Champion (an average length slightly under that of the
Dudleys). He eventually defeated MVP to win the US
Championship, the highest honor of Hardy's WWE tenure. He
held the title for 84 days. One of my favorite things about this
list is that it puts a more positive spin on the careers of guys like
Matt Hardy and similar "other halves" of tag teams that saw
their partners achieve greater singles success. He is in the top
34% of all champions of the WrestleMania Era.

#66: Owen Hart

2-time WWE Intercontinental Champion; 4-time WWE Tag Team
Champion

Every year as WrestleMania Season approaches, the
debate begins about who deserves to go into the WWE Hall of
Fame someday. A name that pops up frequently is Owen Hart.
I usually ignore any and all arguments made against his
inclusion. I think it's ridiculous to suggest he's not a worthy
candidate. There may not be a more historically undervalued

talent than the youngest Hart brother; and his championship accolades reflect it. During the New Generation, Owen basically ran the Tag Team Championship division. For six months in 1995, Hart combined with Yokozuna to dominate the scene as champions. For eight months between 1996 and 1997, Hart teamed with brother-in-law, The British Bulldog, to carry the division as titleholders. Owen Hart is the 5th most successful tag team wrestler in WWE history. Add in his 132 days as the Intercontinental Champion during a time when he was (and could have more often been) a cyclical headlining act and there is no question that Owen should be in the Hall of Fame.

#65: Seth Rollins

1-time WWE World Heavyweight Champion; 1-time WWE United States Champion; 1-time WWE Tag Team Champion

After flirting with having just one World Championship for about eight months from December 2001 to September 2002, Vince McMahon's company finally unified the WWE and World Heavyweight Championships for good in December 2013. With that decision came a heightened level of prestige for whoever rose to hold the Undisputed Title. At *WrestleMania 31*, Seth Rollins cashed in his Money in the Bank contract and captured the belt in a monumental moment, then proceeded to become the first full-blown heel character to hold the World Championship for 210 days or longer since JBL a decade prior. WWE has been a babyface's world for nearly all of its existence, so to have an antagonist reign as the #1 guy for so long has been a historical anomaly. Rollins has seemingly confirmed his spot in WWE's upper echelon as a result. As he, his former S.H.I.E.L.D. mates, and Bray Wyatt have emerged as the foundational stars of the Reality Era's present and future, expectations have developed that suggest Rollins and Co. will all eventually join the ranks of the championship elite.

On a personal note, if pro wrestlers create works of art on the 20'X20' canvas, then Shawn Michaels is pro wrestling's greatest artist. I'll be honest in stating that I found it highly unlikely that anyone capable of knocking him off of that pedestal would ever emerge. Rollins is so good that he has me rethinking that stance.

#64: Wade Barrett
5-time WWE Intercontinental Champion

There have been 19 Intercontinental Champions since Big Show ended the longest single reign of the last decade by Cody Rhodes at *WrestleMania XXVIII*. Of those 19, only two have held the strap for more than 100 days; one of them is Wade Barrett. 25% of the time between April 2012 and August 2015, Barrett has been the IC Champion. In fact, if you look at this decade as of *Summerslam '15*, Barrett's total combination of 397 days as reigning IC titleholder make him the face of the division since 2010. His closest competition is Dolph Ziggler, who has held the strap for a hundred less days total. There might be a tendency to place an asterisk next to such an achievement given the perception of the IC Title not being that important anymore, but I think it speaks to the overall increased quality of the division that talents such as Barrett and Ziggler – who many feel are destined to become the most underutilized main-event-caliber stars of their era – have held the gold for 32% of the decade, thus far. It could be (and has been at times) worse for the division.

#63: Stevie Ray
10-time WCW Tag Team Champion

By a wide margin, Harlem Heat won more Tag Team Championships than any other team in NWA/WCW history. However, if it bothers you that Stevie Ray's place at the roundtable was shaped by the quantity of his tag team gold, then also consider that Harlem Heat were the third longest combined reigning champions (by team) of NWA/WCW lore, as well (individually, Stevie Ray ranks 11th). So, he and his brother, Booker T, are one of the most decorated tag teams of all-time. Hopefully, works like this one will help keep the spirit of NWA/WCW accomplishments alive and well as time passes. WWE's hype machine and the people who (fairly) shape their opinions on WWE's propaganda do not seem to account much for the losing half of the Monday Night War in their historical perspectives. Not on my watch. Harlem Heat is a strong contender to be among the top 10 tag teams of the WrestleMania Era, backed up by their championship track record if by nothing else.

#62: Roddy Piper
1-time WWE Intercontinental Champion; 3-time WCW United States Champion; 1-time WWE Tag Team Champion

The glaring omission of a World Heavyweight Title aside, Roddy Piper is a little bit more successful in wrestling championship lore than he is given credit for. It's all a matter of perspective, I suppose. For one of the Top 30 stars of the WrestleMania Era, his title cupboard is a tad bit bare. As you'll soon be made aware, there are a handful of stars that don't even sniff the Top 90 overall that are ranked ahead of Hot Rod in this discussion. However, what Piper did accomplish should not be made light of. In WWE, he had just the lone Intercontinental Championship run, but he is the 25th ranked wrestler in history for combined number of days as United States Champion. His three reigns over 7 ½ months in WCW significantly boosted his profile as a mainstream titleholder. Roddy will always be remembered more for his words than the variety of championships that adorned the walls of his home office, but it's important to remember with him (and others like him who never won the World title) what he did accomplish.

#61: Greg "The Hammer" Valentine
1-time WWE Intercontinental Champion; 1-time NWA United
States Champion; 1-time WWE Tag Team Champion

Greg Valentine was a dominant upper mid-card force
during the first three years of the WrestleMania Era, holding the
IC Title in WWE and the US Title in the NWA for a combined 300
days between November '83 and September '84 and later
holding the WWE Tag Team Championships for 226 days
between August '85 and April '86. In fact, of the WWE wrestlers
who peaked between the original *Starrcade* and *WrestleMania
2* but who never won the World Championship, The Hammer
was the most successful champion. As alluded to in *The
WrestleMania Era*, Valentine was seemingly picked by Vince
McMahon to provide a more old school base for the
Intercontinental Title division while massively experimenting
with a new age philosophy for Hulk Hogan as his top overall
star; it provided an important dichotomatical contrast for the
fledgling WWE product. Of course, Hammer was also a pillar for
the United States Title division in the NWA, even though just 15
days of his three reigns dating back to 1980 fit the timeframe
chosen for this project (the first day of which included his iconic
Dog Collar match against Roddy Piper at the first *Starrcade*).

#60: MVP
2-time WWE United States Champion; 1-time WWE Tag Team
Champion

If Barrett and Ziggler are destined to be regarded as two
of the most underutilized main-event caliber talents of their era,
then surely MVP has to be considered one of the most
underutilized main-event caliber talents of his era. Under
serious consideration for the Top 90 in *The WrestleMania Era*
first edition, MVP debuted in WWE with the perfect gimmick at
the perfect time. It was perhaps the height of the prima donna
wide receiver in the National Football League and MVP burst

onto the scene reminding many of Terrell Owens and Chad (Ochocinco) Johnson. The character just flat out worked. The man behind the persona was an extremely talented wrestler who made his mark with a dazzling mid-card run between 2007 and 2009 at a time when having a dazzling mid-card run was no easy task. He had a memorable storyline with Matt Hardy and reigned as United States Champion during that period for a modern record 419 days (343 days of which occurred in one noteworthy run that – considering how little Dean Ambrose actually did with the US title in 351 days – ought to be regarded as the greatest under the WWE banner). Unfortunately, his career never progressed. In the Brand Split Era, that was colossally disappointing. MVP was a baller.

#59: Ricky "The Dragon" Steamboat

1-time NWA World Heavyweight Champion; 1-time WWE Intercontinental Champion; 2-time NWA/WCW United States Champion; 3-time NWA/WCW Tag Team Champion

Timing is such a fascinating element of pro wrestling success to consider, as it is with any elite athletic endeavor. In pro basketball discussions, fans and historians often ask what the NBA landscape might have looked like had Michael Jordan not taken a two year hiatus; what might the career of Hakeem Olajuwon, winner of the two championships in Jordan's absence, look like on paper without those elusive rings? He's certainly not as legitimate a Top 10 ever candidate. Timing is a delicate thing that when falling one man's way (or vice versa) can forever alter the perception of his career. Ricky Steamboat is always going to be remembered as a former World Heavyweight Champion. Without that brief run with the big gold belt in WCW, he would be right there with Piper, Rude, and Perfect as one of the greatest stars of his era to never win the big one. He famously dropped the Intercontinental Championship in WWE to Honky Tonk Man, after a very brief title reign, allegedly because he showed commitment to his family and wanted to take time off to be with his newborn son.

What if WWE learns of that intention 65 days earlier? Does The Dragon still win the IC Title at *WrestleMania III*? If he doesn't, how does that change the complexion of the match? And without that match, does the Steamer have the credibility to go back to WCW and win the NWA Championship? Timing, ladies and gentlemen...how fascinating?

#58: Lance Storm
1-time WWE Intercontinental Champion; 3-time WCW United States Champion; 4-time WWE Tag Team Champion

For the period of time when Lance Storm was a top mid-carder, nobody who held a mid-card championship felt safe. Title changes were nearly as common as the turn of a calendar. Take the WCW United States Title as an example. Storm first won it in July 2000 and, from then until WCW closed its doors the following March, there were eight more title changes. Over in WWE, title switching was just as common an epidemic. Storm won the IC Title in July 2001; the title changed hands 10 times over the next year. During the year that followed Storm's first WWE Tag Team Championship victory in 2002, those belts changed hands nine times. So, Lance didn't exactly come of age in an era of lengthy mid-card title runs. However, he was a very good wrestler and an underrated straightforward heel who racked up 8 titles in three highly productive mainstream years in the business. There was a knock on him for being boring, but let him take solace in the fact that far more charismatic individuals accomplished a lot less.

#57: Barry Windham
1-time WCW United States Champion; 2-time WWE Tag Team Champion; 4-time NWA/WCW Tag Team Champion

One of the goals of my first book was to promote the career of Barry Windham as one of the greatest that nobody ever talks about anymore. A bonafide main-event star without the championship accolades to support that status, he joins names like Piper, Rude, Hall, and Hennig as amongst the greatest to have never won the World Heavyweight Championship (though he did win the NWA version after it became secondary to the rechristened WCW Title in the early 1990s). I remember getting emails from fans that started watching pro wrestling during WWE's New Generation or beyond questioning Windham's inclusion in the Four Horsemen induction to the WWE Hall of Fame in 2012. I immediately abandoned the writing schedule I'd been keeping and wrote Barry Windham's chapter for *The WrestleMania Era* to take advantage of the internal fire lit from those fans not having enough appreciation for what he did in the business. It goes back to the WWE-led mission to glorify the Monday Night Wars but largely ignore the 1980s conflicts that led to it. It was the NWA in the late 1980s that best showcased the well-rounded talents of Barry Windham. His 9 ½ month United States Title reign is one of the longest ever and his six combined Tag Team Championships across WWE and NWA/WCW puts him in rarified air as well. So, let it never be forgotten how good Barry Windham was or how much he accomplished.

#56: Ivan and Nikita Koloff

1-time NWA United States Champion; 3-time NWA Tag Team Champions

As mentioned in *The WrestleMania Era*, I grew up watching the National Wrestling Alliance in the Carolinas and, in studying NWA history, I had a hard time separating Ivan and Nikita Koloff. They had profound impacts on each other's personal and professional lives, with Ivan bringing Nikita to Jim Crockett Promotions and Nikita stimulating Ivan's path to born-again Christianity (Ivan is now an ordained minister). So, to me, they're inseparable in hindsight despite each having substantial careers apart. "The Russians," as they were known, are quite possibly the greatest ever example of how to work an anti-

American gimmick – to live and breathe it to the point that it's in your bones. Nikita lived it so much that he learned to speak Russian and changed his legal name to reflect his wrestling name. Together, the Koloffs combined for a pair of NWA Tag Team Championships; and there was no more important Tag Team Title in pro wrestling lore than the NWA Tag straps circa the 1980s. Ivan added a third reign with a different partner and, though his WWE Championship victory was not counted for this list due to it taking place outside the WM Era, Nikita's 5th longest reign in history as the United States Champion was a major reason for their placement in the 70th percentile.

#55: Ron Simmons
1-time WCW World Heavyweight Champion; 1-time WCW Tag Team Champion; 3-time WWE Tag Team Champion

The first-ever black World Heavyweight Champion, Ron Simmons is one of history's most underrated figures. As an All-American at Florida State University, he was also one of wrestling lore's most accomplished athletes to make a career of performing on the 20'X20' canvas. Outside of Kurt Angle and Brock Lesnar, is there a more successful athlete to make the transition to pro wrestling? Simmons also boasts another important distinction as one half of the longest reigning WCW Tag Team Champions in history. Demolition is celebrated for their record reign in WWE and rightfully so, but the WCW equivalent – Doom – has never been as heralded. Doom put Simmons on the map, giving him the freedom to hone his craft en route to becoming a WCW headliner in 1991 and winning the WCW Championship in 1992. He later replicated his tag team success in WWE as one half of the APA, who combined for three reigns as champions.

#54: Mr. Perfect
2-time WWE Intercontinental Champion; 1-time WCW United States Champion; 1-time WCW Tag Team Champion

Not many wrestlers can say that they held the top secondary championship in both of the promotions widely recognized as the most substantial in history; a very few can say that they held those titles for 17 total months or longer. Though that track record is far from perfect – nobody's is in pro wrestling – only one of the men to achieve such honors was ever good enough to be given the moniker of "Perfect" : Mr. Perfect, to be exact, Curt Hennig. Mr. Perfect was arguably the Intercontinental Championship's greatest titleholder. As much as Randy Savage is justifiably credited for building the belt's reputation through his masterpiece with Ricky Steamboat at *WrestleMania III* and Honky Tonk Man is placed on a historical pedestal for being the title's longest reigning champion, Hennig should be credited for the IC Title becoming the "worker's championship" that so many great wrestlers (Bret Hart, Shawn Michaels, and Chris Jericho to name a very few) once pegged as the ultimate achievement for their careers. Hennig was the perfect Intercontinental Champion, a character strong enough to keep the belt on-par with the World Championship and a performer capable of having the best match on any card. His United States and Tag Team Title reigns in WCW boosted his profile.

#53: Rick Steiner

1-time WCW United States Champion; 2-time WWE Tag Team Champion; 8-time NWA/WCW Tag Team Champion

A strong argument can be made that The Steiner Brothers were the greatest tag team ever. Pro Wrestling Illustrated once ranked them the 2nd greatest of all-time. With nine Tag Team Championship runs in WWE and NWA/WCW as a duo, the Steiners rank behind only The Dudley Boyz in total title reigns for one unit. Rick Steiner, himself, ranks fourth in the WrestleMania Era in the total number of days (680) reigned as a Tag Team Champion, putting him behind only Demolition, Kane, and Billy Gunn. So, essentially, we're talking about a fixture in the mainstream wrestling scene for over a decade. It could be just me – I put Scott, by himself, into the all-time Top 90 in my book – but there's nary a conversation to be had in the last ten years about The Dog-Faced Gremlin. Is it a reflection of the modern inconsequence of the tag team division? Is it a disregard of NWA/WCW history? For whatever reason, Rick's is not a name you hear much. Hopefully, we're reaching a point where that can change. WWE are the gatekeepers of pro wrestling lore right now and they are beginning to relent on their once constant barrage on WCW historically. It's time we all took notice of not just the World Championship-winning member of The Steiner Brothers, but of his older brother too.

#52: John Morrison
3-time WWE Intercontinental Champion; 5-time WWE Tag Team Champion

Not far behind on the list of the WrestleMania Era's most successful tag team wrestlers is John Morrison, whose 657 total days as a WWE Tag Team Champion are less than a month off of Steiner's pace. JoMo is the only man in the modern age, in fact, to hold the Tag Team Titles for nearly 300 days or longer with two different tag team partners. Considering when he was dominant in the division, it could thus be argued that Morrison carried the WWE Tag Team scene between 2005 and 2009. No matter in this case that the division was historically weak during that period, for Morrison was never weak; those years saw him rise the ranks to becoming a consistent Intercontinental Championship threat, a 3-time IC Champion for a combined 209 days, and eventually even a World Heavyweight Title contender during the final year of his WWE run. Was he a beneficiary of the Brand Extension's greater number of championships to attain? Absolutely, but he was also one of the most uniquely gifted in-ring performers of his time; let his title record reflect *that* rather than when he won them.

#51: "Ravishing" Rick Rude
1-time WWE Intercontinental Champion; 1-time WCW United States Champion; 1-time NWA Tag Team Champion

It is thanks to men like Rick Rude and Mr. Perfect that I feel the Title Formula is justified in its effectiveness. In between them on this list sit two wrestlers who won at least 8 titles each and join Rude and Hennig on the roster of men who never held the World Championship. Yet, with half or less title accolades, Rude and Perfect still sandwich that more heavily golden-clad pair. Rude accomplished his track record on the back of the second longest United States Championship reign of all-time. He joins Lex Luger as the only two men who ever held the US Title for a year or more in a single reign and is the last of the six men who have ever held the two top mainstream mid-card championships (along with WWE's Intercontinental) for a year or more in total. Of course, he was a noteworthy IC Champion who won the title in a headlining match at *WrestleMania V* and dropped it in an equally high profile match at *Summerslam '89*. His six months as NWA Tag Team Champion with Manny Fernandez round out his title achievements. What a legend...

#50: "Sycho" Sid
2-time WWE Champion; 2-time WCW World Heavyweight Champion; 1-time WCW United States Champion

Sid is a great example of the historical benefits afforded by winning the World Heavyweight Championship; he is also a great example of why so many categories need be accounted for in shaping an all-time ranking system. Though the total combined length of all his title reigns (WWE, WCW, and US included) were half the length of Rude's US Championship reign, Sid ranks ahead because of the established value of the World Title. The business has become all about winning it; a fact that some dislike even though they struggle to dispute it. Sid's place in pro wrestling lore is shaped heavily by being a 4-time World

Champion. It may get him into the Hall of Fame ahead of his more talented peers, despite all four of his reigns coming during a tumultuous time in the business (HBK's attitude and health, WCW's dying day ineptness, etc.). Still, he's got an impressive trophy case.

#49: Yokozuna
2-time WWE Champion; 1-time WWE Tag Team Champion

Of course, the benefits of being a World Champion are magnified if you hold it for any length of time. Such is the situation with Yokozuna, who reigned as WWE Champion from June 1993 to *WrestleMania X* in March 1994 (280 days). He's tied with JBL for the 15th longest combined number of days as WWE Champion since 1984. Add in his 175 day reign as Tag Team Champion (with Owen Hart) and the Samoan Hall of Famer might be one of the most underrated titleholders of the WrestleMania Era. Much goes into the conversation of greatness. Intangible qualities such as the legitimacy of a championship reign should not be ignored. Yokozuna was very believable in his role; beating him meant something. It's nice to see him ranked in a spot that accurately reflects his place in pro wrestling lore.

#48: Cody Rhodes
2-time WWE Intercontinental Champion; 6-time WWE Tag Team Champion

It's interesting to note – via cases like Cody Rhodes and John Morrison – what a little bit of longevity and borderline-headlining talent can earn members of the modern era as compared to their more renowned peers of yesteryear. It certainly says something about Rhodes that he is the only man to hold the Intercontinental Championship for over 200 days in the last decade. He is the IC Title division's modern outlier, his reign skewing the data that shapes the average title reign length since 2005. He is the man that brought back the classic belt, citing a return to the championship's glory days. There were times when it seemed he might use the belt as a springboard to main-event stardom in the same ways that Savage, Bret, HBK, and others popularized. Though he has bookended his career to date with successful runs in the tag team scene – 16 months combined reigns as Tag Team Champion with Goldust, Drew McIntyre, Hardcore Holly, and Ted DiBiase Jr – he's young enough and skilled enough to climb higher up WWE's hierarchy again. Scary to think that a few more title reigns and perhaps one day a World Championship if he's very fortunate and Cody Rhodes could wind up one of the most successful stars of the WrestleMania Era. It's not that far-fetched.

#47: Goldberg

1-time WWE World Heavyweight Champion; 1-time WCW World Heavyweight Champion; 2-time WCW United States Champion; 1-time WCW Tag Team Champion

If there is a better characterization in pro wrestling history of the phrase "lightning in a bottle" than Bill Goldberg, please point him/her out to me. It took him 18 months in WCW to accumulate his entire golden trophy case, including a six month reign as WCW Champion. In WWE, it took him less than six months to become World Heavyweight Champion. Goldberg was a phenomenon. We can see that here. Five major mainstream championships in two years worth of work and the #47 spot in the WrestleMania Era ranking of greatest titleholders. Unfortunately, Goldberg's statistics fail to capture in the record books the kinds of statements that men like Arn Anderson have made about him over the years, such as him being on equal footing as some of the hottest acts to have ever graced the wrestling business (Hogan, Austin, Rock, etc.). So, that needs to be brought up in these conversations; it serves as an example of why we need to broaden our scope of criterion for these "greatest of all-time" discussions.

#46: Alberto Del Rio
4-time WWE World Heavyweight Champion

In baseball, statistics have come under fire in the last decade for their inflation associated with steroid and other performance enhancing drug use by the players. Pundits often question how history will view the so-called "Steroid Era" accordingly. In wrestling, there have been many eras during which titles frequently changed hands; that has been discussed already. The World Championship has not been immune to these promotional games of hot potato, hence the need for a Title Formula to find a statistical balance between eras. What needs to be explored now is the period of decreased emphasis on the Brand Extension which led to a more lax attitude toward the pair of World Championships and, ultimately, the value of the World Heavyweight Title in WWE being reduced to the status of the Intercontinental Championship circa early-to-mid-1990s (its average reign was cut from four months after Batista's 9 ½ month reign ended in 2006 to a very mid-card title-like two months).

Alberto Del Rio, then, was arguably one of the greatest beneficiaries of his respective time. You could be excused for failing to remember that he was ever WWE Champion (he held it twice for 84 days); he was a plot device in the ongoing saga between John Cena and CM Punk. Not to take anything away from his in-ring ability, but his connection with the audience much better fit his time as World Heavyweight Champion (twice for 223 days) when it was more akin to the IC Title of yesteryear. Time will tell if Del Rio becomes a glaring outlier in this current position. Will modern era stars stick out like sore thumbs because one company, for many years, had two titles for each division?

#45: John "Bradshaw" Layfield

1-time WWE Champion; 1-time WWE Intercontinental Champion; 1-time WWE United States Champion; 3-time WWE Tag Team Champion

There's a certain sense of irony in JBL and ADR being positioned back-to-back on the greatest champions list considering that, when Del Rio debuted, comparisons were instantly made of him to Bradshaw. In 2004, JBL – like ADR in 2010 – came out of nowhere to emerge as a top guy. As Bradshaw, John Layfield experienced marginal success as a 3-time Tag Team Champion during the division's second golden era. And then, BOOM!, he was a top guy. Nobody has ever made the transition faster from mid-carder-for-life status to WWE Champion – just three months for the massive makeover to become so successful that it yielded a 280 day reign as "The Man" on Smackdown. Fortunately, he was ready for the challenge, won over his critics by year's end, and earned a WrestleMania headlining match for his efforts. Low and behold, JBL ended his career as one of the rare talents in the modern era to personify the old adage that "the man makes the title." Neither the US or IC Championships were extremely coveted at the time that Layfield challenged for them, but his reigns with those belts elevated them both; they were a bigger deal by association with JBL.

#44: Goldust

3-time WWE Intercontinental Champion; 2-time WWE United States Champion; 3-time WWE Tag Team Champion; 2-time WCW Tag Team Champion

One of the best things about the Title Formula is that, especially in a day and age when never advancing beyond the mid-card is frowned upon by many pundits, careers that peaked with the Intercontinental or United States Championships are validated. Goldust is a prime example. He has not headlined a

PPV singles match since 1996 and he never sniffed a World Title, but here he sits on the list ahead of several former World Champions and Hall of Famers. It's OK, to borrow from Samuel 'Plan's outstanding book, *101 WWE Matches To See Before You Die*, to be more responsible for making the show than stealing it or being it. Goldust's 5 reigns as a mid-card singles champion for a total of 397 days and 5 reigns as Tag Team Champion (with Cody Rhodes, Booker T, Barry Windham, and Ricky Steamboat) for a total of 305 days stand as testament that a Hall of Fame career can be built in the modern era on the back of superlative work somewhere beyond the main-event.

#43: Vader
3-time WCW World Heavyweight Champion; 1-time WCW United States Champion

So many discussions on social media lead to really interesting questions. Not long ago, I was having a conversation about things in the past that would work in the present and someone asked me on Twitter something along the lines of "If you could bring a certain wrestler's style from days gone by to the current product, whose would it be?" I needed a few days to ponder my answer, but I eventually settled on Vader circa 1992-1994 in WCW. The stylistic sense that shaped my response was predicated less on the bruising, stiff brawler-type that Vader perhaps best characterized and more on the idea of a wrestler who combined those "real fighter" traits with the ability to do things in a wrestling ring that nobody his size should've been able to do. Vader was a perfectly sized monster for his time, but he could fly. The current WWE roster member settled upon to bring those unique characteristics to WWE circa 2015 was Luke Harper. I would be thrilled to see Harper, a favorite of nearly anyone with a mind for the business, replicate half the success that Vader enjoyed as a former United States Champion and a year-long holder of the WCW Championship over three total reigns.

#42: The New Age Outlaws
2-time WWE Intercontinental Champions; 11-time WWE Tag Team Champions

The New Age Outlaws are perhaps the most legendary tag team of the WrestleMania Era. Billy Gunn's golden trophy case features more championships than Road Dogg's, but much like with the Koloffs from the 1980s, it's virtually impossible to separate Jesse James from Mr. Ass. The D-Oh-Double G won all of his Tag Team Championships with Gunn, who is the most successful tag team wrestler of the WrestleMania Era with a combined 952 days between reigns with James and Bart Gunn. It's quite possible that nobody will ever accumulate the total success of Billy Gunn in the tag team division; his closest competition (Kane) is over 200 days behind him on the list. Both Gunn and Dogg had a cup of coffee with the Intercontinental Championship too, edging them ahead of a few of their peers who won the World Title on the all-time ranking of greatest champions. It was a reflection of their status during the Attitude Era that they earned the company's top secondary title.

#41: Shelton Benjamin
3-time WWE Intercontinental Champion; 1-time WWE United States Champion; 2-time WWE Tag Team Champion

Shelton Benjamin is one of my favorite wrestlers to have never won the World Title. He is probably the closest thing we got during the Brand Split Era to a Greg Valentine, Tito Santana-type titleholder whose lasting reputation was forged solely through work as an outstanding mid-card wrestler. As the longest reigning combined holder of the United States and Intercontinental Championships of the 21st century (594 days total), Benjamin was perhaps WWE's top role player of modern times. He could be counted on to credibly uphold the historical status of the titles, combine with legends like HBK, Angle, HHH, and Y2J for classic matches, and employ his uncanny athleticism to raise the bar in Ladder matches. He was also one of the most respected Tag Team Champions of last decade despite relatively limited time spent in the division (The World's Greatest Tag Team was just that good). Like Goldust, his career is arguably Hall of Fame worthy and he never came close to winning the World Championship or main-eventing a PPV. That's a noteworthy achievement.

#40: Rob Van Dam

1-time WWE Champion; 6-time WWE Intercontinental Champion; 3-time WWE Tag Team Champion

If Shelton Benjamin had ever been as over as Rob Van Dam, then he too would've been a World Champion in WWE. Alas, few athletes have ever been as over as RVD without consistent opportunities to express themselves on the microphone. Van Dam cut a single memorable promo in his entire WWE career (at ECW's *One Night Stand*), but that mysterious "it" is not defined by one attribute alone. Because RVD was so uniquely gifted between the ropes (with a boost from the best air-brushed tights in the business), he got over in a hurry and never looked back, culminating in his brief run with the WWE Title in 2006. For the rest of his storied run, he was one of the ultimate utility wrestlers, placed in whatever role needed a super over upper-card act. It was in that role that he briefly held the Intercontinental Championship 6-times (barely over a month on average) and the Tag Team Championships 3-times (with Kane, Booker T, and Rey Mysterio).

#39: Diamond Dallas Page

3-time WCW World Heavyweight Champion; 2-time WCW United States Champion; 4-time WCW Tag Team Champion; 1-time WWE Tag Team Champion

Has there been a more underrated main-event career than that of Diamond Dallas Page? Call him a victim of WWE's revisionist history that undersells the value of WCW perhaps. If that's the case, let's rectify it.

Just a short while ago, we brought JBL's meteoric rise into focus. Certainly, Layfield might well be WWE's most prominent mid-card rags to main-event riches story. Yet, it pales in comparison to Dallas Page. To go from uber fan driving a pink Cadillac to the ring at *WrestleMania VI* to a WCW manager to feuding with Randy Savage to headlining celebrity angles with Hulk Hogan to winning every major WCW Championship over a decade-long span is one of wrestling lore's finest examples of hard work paying off. DDP was hell bent on getting in the ring and making something of himself. He was a student of the game on par with Triple H, never failing to put the time in to achieve his goals...and he achieved more than he could have ever imagined. Sure, his 3 WCW Championship reigns combined for a paltry 29 days (there you go, Mick Foley; you don't hold the record for shortest length of time over three title runs). In fact, his 10 major titles do not add up to even half the combined number of reigning days as Benjamin's US and IC title runs alone. Such statistics are used by his critics to knock his success, just as Mick Foley's stats are used to try and lessen his historical impact. I say, in the cases of Foley and DDP, those figures matter very little. One is a Hall of Famer and the other will be before it's all said and done. Bang on that.

#38: Mick Foley
3-time WWE Champion; 8-time WWE Tag Team Champion; 1-time WCW Tag Team Champion

Do we even need to do the obligatory pat on the back for Mick Foley like we did for DDP?

If you have paid attention to WWE for any reasonable length of time and you haven't yet developed a great appreciation for what the Three Faces of Foley brought to pro wrestling, then I don't know what to tell you; maybe read a book or listen to the way that (most of) his peers talk about him. He's not my favorite wrestler by any means, but there's no wrestler who I respect more. That being said, he held eleven championships in WWE for a combined seven months. He has one of the worst ratios of World Titles won to combined World Title reign length in history; the only wrestler with a minimum of three reigns to have a worse ratio is, as just mentioned, DDP. In WWE lore, only Undertaker and Rock have more pathetic ratios for Tag Team Championships. Foley's eight reigns averaged 21 days in length (Taker's is 13 days and Rock's is a dreadful 5 days). Nevertheless, he still won a lot of titles, including the richest prize in the business that boosted his golden profile all the way to the Top 40.

#37: Eddie Guerrero

1-time WWE Champion; 2-time WWE Intercontinental Champion; 1-time WWE United States Champion; 1-time WCW United States Champion; 4-time WWE Tag Team Champion

Eddie Guerrero had the modern classic pro wrestling career. He started as a mid-card wrestler, winning numerous mid-card wrestling championships, most notably the United States and Intercontinental Titles twice each. He was so good and got so over that he eventually earned a main-event position, defeating Brock Lesnar for the WWE Championship in February 2004 and holding it 4 ½ months. If you most appreciate wrestling for its biggest stars, then this might not ring as true for you as it does for others; for me, as a thirty year fan, few moments mean as much as the ones that see long-time veterans who just kept scratching and clawing their way to the top actually reach the peak of the mountain to win the World Championship. Guerrero winning the WWE Title was wrestling's version of Dirk Nowitzki finally winning the NBA Finals. There's nothing like those moments and they don't happen often, so make sure to appreciate them when they do.

#36: Sheamus
3-time WWE World Heavyweight Champion; 2-time WWE United States Champion

I took a lot of heat in the 1st edition of *The WrestleMania Era* for ranking Sheamus in the second tier of the all-time Top 90. Yet, I maintain it was for good reason. Though I dropped him back to the top member of the third tier in the 2nd edition, it takes merely a quick scan of the Celtic Warrior's statistics to understand the method behind his ambitiously ranked historical stature. Take his golden trophy case, for instance; Sheamus was the last dominant World Heavyweight Champion before the belt was unified with the WWE Title, holding the belt for 210 days. Add in his two reigns as WWE Champion and he has held a World Title 20% of the time in his five year career (and he's held a title of some sort for 33% of his career). You can call him overrated, a lousy babyface, or stupid-looking, but The Great White has had a very good run in WWE to date; the rest of his resume reflects the same kind of success as seen here.

#35: Brock Lesnar
4-time WWE World Heavyweight Champion

It's not often that you will see a Top 50 all-time champion's resume be built solely on one category of championship, but it should come as no surprise that one of the few extraordinary cases is that of the extremely extraordinary Brock Lesnar. 579 days is the length of time that he has spent as the top titleholder. During the WrestleMania Era, only five men in WWE have held the World Title longer than The Beast Incarnate. From the moment he stepped foot in WWE, Lesnar has conquered the main-event scene with his unique set of skills. He was WWE Champion before he'd been on the main roster for six months. He bypassed any sort of "due-paying" process on the hierarchical ladder and has rarely ever competed for any title besides the top prize. What's scary is that his title stats are, along with longevity, his two weakest historical categories and he's still a Top 20 minimum all-time guy. I don't know about you, but I'm glad we've got him in WWE for another few years.

#34: Rey Mysterio

3-time WWE World Heavyweight Champion; 2-time WWE Intercontinental Champion; 4-time WWE Tag Team Champion; 3-time WCW Tag Team Champion

It was mentioned a few pages ago how we should appreciate the hard-working veterans getting to the top. Rey Mysterio accomplished that feat during a time when I think we were getting spoiled by the frequency of the phenomenon. The trend began in the 1990s when ten year veterans like Bret Hart, HBK, Stone Cold, and Mick Foley made good, but there was some space in between the occurrences. From 2004 to 2006, it was happening all the time. Eddie did it, then Benoit, then Mysterio, and then RVD. It's something that I think we collectively appreciate more the greater the distance that there is between two occasions. I'm not sure that Mysterio's is remembered as fondly as it would have been had Benoit and Guerrero not just accomplished it a couple of years before (not to mention the popular, internet-driven, so-called Eddie-themed reasons for it occurring at all). For anyone who buys into the "Mysterio won the title because Eddie died" theory, it should serve as validation for Rey that he won the title twice more this decade. Though always a briefly reigning champion no matter the division he was captaining as titleholder, he worked his tail off and succeeded.

#33: Scott Steiner

1-time WCW World Heavyweight Champion; 2-time WCW United States Champion; 2-time WWE Tag Team Champion; 7-time NWA/WCW Tag Team Champion

When I wrote *The WrestleMania Era*, one of the themes of the project as it moved further along in its process was caretaking history for wrestlers that were no longer recognized by WWE (no matter the reason) for their considerable achievements. Scott Steiner was among that group. You ask WWE fans who have been watching since, say, *WrestleMania X8* or later about Scott Steiner and you can forgive them for thinking immediately about the botchfest with Triple H that stunk out Boston at *Royal Rumble 2003*. He's been a pariah ever since, his stellar body of work from 2001 and prior swept under the proverbial rug. Big Poppa Pump was probably one of the most controversially ranked stars in my book to those that knew little of his NWA/WCW career, but Steiner's track record is outstanding. He's one of the greatest tag team wrestlers ever. A 9-time champion in both WWE and WCW, he eventually adopted the Freakzilla persona and became a singles star. His nearly six months as US Champion preceded his four month run as WCW World Heavyweight Champion – the last WCW Title reign in the company's history and one that, quite frankly, lived up to the standard set by the best of the NWA. So, don't forget about Scott Steiner; he had a career worth remembering.

#32: Daniel Bryan

4-time WWE World Heavyweight Champion; 1-time WWE Intercontinental Champion; 1-time WWE United States Champion; 1-time WWE Tag Team Champion

In regards to the Title Formula, one of the things that I have thought about doing (and still may eventually do) is eliminating one day or less title reigns. As a 30 year fan, I find the idea of the single day reign sort of despicable in the majority of cases. Here's the thing, though: if I were to strike title reigns that are better described by hours than days/weeks/months, then we'd lose the ability to properly contextualize certain careers. Take Daniel Bryan, for example. He has technically been WWE Champion three times, even though he only ever really held the title one time because his first reign lasted a few minutes and his second from one night to the next. Strip him of those two reigns and he's, by virtue of his golden trophy case, no greater a star in the modern era than Cody Rhodes. And, while there should be a logical gap between Bryan and Rhodes, the point still stands that giving Bryan credit for two cups of coffee with the WWE Championship perhaps unfairly skews the overall perception of his place in wrestling lore. What do you think? Nevertheless, Bryan held every title there was to hold in the world's preeminent wrestling federation and, Yes!, he deserves plenty of historical credit for it.

#31: The Ultimate Warrior
1-time WWE Champion; 2-time WWE Intercontinental Champion

Going back to something I mentioned very early on about Howard Finkel's introductions, there's not any wrestler's intro that I mimic (to this day) more than Ultimate Warrior's. "THEE...ULLLLLL-Ta Mat – WAR Eeyore!!" I'm always happy to have a reason to rank Warrior highly on a list, for no wrestler captured my youthful imagination more as a kid. Warrior was my Hogan. His 10 month reign as WWE Champion completed my conversion from a predominantly NWA/WCW fan to a mostly WWE fan. That one, 293 day run has been good enough to keep him in the Top 20 all-time for total time spent as WWE Champion. His 432 days over two reigns as Intercontinental Champion have stayed the course as 6th greatest ever, as well. The Hall of Famer amassed in just three combined title reigns what it has taken other wrestlers a dozen title reigns to achieve. Such was the power of the WAR-YAHHHHHH.

#30: Kofi Kingston

4-time WWE Intercontinental Champion; 3-time WWE United States Champion; 5-time WWE Tag Team Champion

We're going to blink and Kofi Kingston will have been around for over a decade; that's how fast time flies. It's going to be fascinating to see what kind of legacy he's going to leave. You look at his resume, with twelve championships amassed since late 2008 when he first won the Tag Team Championships with CM Punk, and you assume that he is only going to continue adding to it. Could he become the most decorated mid-card champion of all-time? It's not an illogical assertion. He's almost there as it is and he's just now reaching what I'd regard as a wrestler's prime (when his physical prowess may scale back but is replaced by wisdom and subsequent strength of character). If he retired tomorrow, he'd have held the Intercontinental and United States Championships for 475 days – one of the top 20 marks of the WrestleMania Era. He's also already topped 400 days as a Tag Team Champion.

Kofi, via his title resume, would seem to have put together a quietly underrated career, has he not?

#29: Christian

2-time WWE World Heavyweight Champion; 4-time WWE Intercontinental Champion; 9-time WWE Tag Team Champion

Shortly before writing this, I watched Christian and Edge appear on Steve Austin's WWE Network podcast. Edge was asked if he thought Christian was a sure bet for the Hall of Fame and the Rated R Superstar quickly replied, "Absolutely." To a lot of people that I've spoken with, Christian is a fringe Hall of Famer. I think it's time we all agreed that Edge's response is the one we should affirmate when we talk of Christian's candidacy. He's one of the greatest tag teamers ever, tied for 3rd all-time on the list of wrestlers who held the WWE Tag Team

Championships most in their careers. He was a four-time Intercontinental Champion, as well; and, while he was never a long-reigning IC titleholder, I'd argue that he was memorable in his role each time (I was actually in attendance for two of his four title wins). Then, the icing on the cake was the summer of 2011. People call that period the "Summer of Punk"; it could just as easily be called the "Summer of Christian." As with his IC title runs, his two reigns as World Heavyweight Champion were not long, but they were definitely memorable. There's nothing fringe about Christian's Hall of Fame resume.

#28: Dolph Ziggler

2-time WWE World Heavyweight Champion; 4-time WWE Intercontinental Champion; 1-time WWE United States Champion; 1-time WWE Tag Team Champion

Periodization is a necessary historical exploration that helps us contextualize careers in sports entertainment. Samuel 'Plan discusses this heavily in his excellent book, *101 WWE Matches To See Before You Die*. Without periodization, the Hall of Fame discussion just had about Christian might easily extend to the likes of Dolph Ziggler. The majority of Christian's career is fairly similar in achievement and status as Ziggler and Dolph outranks him on this list, but it was the time that Christian was in his peak mid-card position that separates him. Let's not belittle Ziggler's accomplishments, by any means, but let's simultaneously make it clear that he has a lot more work to do before he even sniffs a mention in the Hall of Fame conversation, despite reigning as World Champion longer than Christian, as a mid-card singles champion for far longer, and even reigning for six days longer as a Tag Team Champion (in one reign versus Christian's seven). Right now, Ziggler looks poised to have a career that looks like similar to Rick Martel, a mid-card specialist who had the chops to perhaps ascend higher and who legitimately – as in not counting Ziggler's half Smackdown as World Heavyweight Champion in February 2011 - held a World Championship (in the AWA) after the belt had been considerably devalued. Will that be good enough for Hall of Fame candidacy some day? Let's see if Martel gets in first...

#27: CM Punk
5-time WWE World Heavyweight Champion; 1-time WWE Intercontinental Champion; 1-time WWE Tag Team Champion

Some people like to say that we need time to put CM Punk's career into proper perspective. I say that's nonsense. Punk is one of the Top 20 WWE Superstars of the WrestleMania Era, statistically. And might I add "easily" for emphasis. You wonder what his resume might look like if there had not been an ECW brand to house his debut and if he had instead been brought to Smackdown. There, he might have been a prime candidate to win the United States Championship in an age when the belt was passed around infrequently. It would have been a nice "stat padder" for the Straight Edge Savior. As far as titles are concerned, Punk was mostly a World Champion during his 2006-2013 career. Obviously, the 434 day reign as WWE Champion is the highlight. The longest single reign since Hulk Hogan's, Punk's run at the top was denigrated by pundits for not always seeing him featured in the last match on PPVs but, in reality, his was a reign that produced as consistent a quality of in-ring product as any title reign in WWE lore. Factor in his four other World Title reigns and CM Punk is the 7th longest reigning World Champion of modern times, bested only by Hogan, Flair, Cena, Hart, Orton, and Triple H.

#26: Scott "Razor Ramon" Hall
4-time WWE Intercontinental Champion; 2-time WCW United States Champion; 7-time WCW Tag Team Champion

Of the six men in the Top 50 Greatest Champions of the WrestleMania Era who never won a World Championship, Scott Hall ranks the highest. I think it's incredibly impressive that Razor managed to best someone like the 5-time World

Champion, Punk, in a statistically-based championship race. From the Title Formula, Hall earned roughly half of his golden accolades in WWE and the other half in WCW. In WWE, he was the first man to hold Intercontinental Title four times. He dominated that division during the New Generation. When he flipped to WCW, he added to his success as the top mid-card singles champion but really made his name as the other half of the Outsiders with Kevin Nash. He ranks 4th in NWA/WCW history as a total combined reigning Tag Team Champion. Odd that he never won the straps in WWE given how natural he was in that role in WCW.

In *The WrestleMania Era*, it was sort of a loose qualification for the Top Tier of the greatest 90 that you had to have won the World Title. On that list, just like this one, Scott Hall has the best statistical title resume of any of the non-World Champions. Though, on that list, he ranks outside the Top 30, I'd call him the greatest of that elusive list of elite talents who never won the WWE or WCW Championships.

#25: Kurt Angle
6-time WWE World Heavyweight Champion; 1-time WWE Intercontinental Champion; 1-time WCW United States Champion; 1-time WWE Tag Team Champion

The Top 25 begins with your Olympic Hero! Oh, it's true! It's damn true!

Kurt Angle had an amazing WWE career, didn't he? He is one of the rare wrestlers that didn't need longevity to fuel his overall championship glory. 2000-2006 was all that it took for Angle to become the 25th most successful champion of the WrestleMania Era. Look who he is surrounded by. Using only the five wrestlers ranked behind and ahead of him, it took them an average of 14 years to put together their title statistics; Angle accomplished nearly as much if not more in half the time. I bring his name up in a similar manner that I do CM Punk's when discussing all-time historical stature. They are both the types that you hope mend fences with WWE so that their careers can be celebrated to the extent that they deserve instead of ignored. I found it slightly bothersome in recent years when WWE would produce Attitude Era documentaries and none of them really talked about Kurt Angle. I would find it similarly irritating a decade from now if WWE produced Reality Era docs and barely mentioned CM Punk. They each played such important roles in WWE lore over the last 20 years.

#24: Jeff Hardy
3-time WWE World Heavyweight Champion; 4-time WWE Intercontinental Champion; 6-time WWE Tag Team Champion; 1-time WCW Tag Team Champion

Not everyone can be a top guy from the start like a Kurt Angle. Remarkable are the instances when a wrestler scratches and claws his way from the bottom to the very top; and no one in WWE lore started from quite the depths as Jeff Hardy. The Enigma was an enhancement talent brought on to do nothing more than bump for and lose to established wrestlers. Somehow, Hardy went from jobber in the mid-1990s to teen heartthrob by the late 1990s and early 2000s as a multi-time Tag Team Champion to a multi-time Intercontinental Champion by the mid-2000s to a multi-time World Champion by the late 2000s. Only DDP can challenge that rags to riches story. It's so astounding that it bears a synonymous reiteration. Other famous top stars have gone from tag success to the ultimate singles prize, but not even Michaels, Hart, Booker, Edge, etc. were jobbers like Jeff Hardy. It's as eye-popping a career resume as exists in industry history: the 24th most accomplished champion of the WrestleMania Era (featuring all the listed accolades)...former WWE jobber. Unbelievable. I hope he lives long enough to give his Hall of Fame induction speech someday.

#23: Kane
2-time WWE World Heavyweight Champion; 2-time WWE Intercontinental Champion; 11-time WWE Tag Team Champion; 1-time WCW Tag Team Champion

Kane's storyline brother, The Undertaker, has set the bar impossibly high for any big man to follow in the future. So, why don't we anoint the Big Red Monster Machine's career as the attainable act to achieve first? If any larger athlete can ever manage to remain relevant long enough to win a pair of World Championships twelve years apart and win fourteen mid-card titles (amidst a slew of ridiculous storylines that only a talent as comfortable in his own skin as Kane could have endured I might add), then perhaps that man could then set his sights on raising the bar above the Phenom.

The bulk of the points earned to place Kane as the 23rd most successful champion came, interestingly, from his 12 Tag Team Championship reigns. For most of his career, he has been a utility headliner, meaning that he very rarely held the top title in WWE, but he competed for it almost every year for seventeen years; they simply plugged him in whenever a WWE or World Heavyweight Champion needed viable opposition. Yet, Kane is the 2nd longest reigning Tag Team Champion of the WrestleMania Era with 721 combined days as a titleholder.

#22: The Undertaker
7-time WWE World Heavyweight Champion; 6-time WWE Tag Team Champion; 1-time WCW Tag Team Champion

How fitting that the Brothers of Destruction are ranked back-to-back…

At the end of the day, a wrestling championship is merely a fictional accolade, but you have to earn the status that a promotion entrusts to a wrestler by giving them a championship. Winning is similar. In order to win consistently in pro wrestling, a superstar must demonstrate a high level of importance to the company's present or future. The Undertaker is the utmost representation of fictional excellence in many ways. In addition to being a distinguished 7-time World Champion and Tag Team Champion, he is also perhaps the greatest winner in sports entertainment lore, highlighted by his untouchable 1991-2014 undefeated Streak on wrestling's grandest stage. He is also the perfect embodiment of the phrase that has meant so much to establishing the viability of pro wrestling in a non-kayfabe world: "suspension of disbelief." The greatest gimmick performer ever, Taker ensures that each one of us who watches him gets into a zone of WWE's fictional construct; he is a "Deadman" after all.

Undertaker means a lot of things to pro wrestling lore; certainly more than his 22nd greatest titleholder ranking could ever do justice.

#21: The Miz
1-time WWE Champion; 4-time WWE Intercontinental Champion; 2-time WWE United States Champion; 5-time WWE Tag Team Champion

Surely, this has to be the most surprising entry on the entire list to the majority of readers, right? The Miz, quite possibly the most reviled WWE Champion of the modern era, ends up ahead of CM Punk (Ha), Undertaker, Daniel Bryan, Kurt Angle, Mick Foley, and the like. Yet, that is the kind of career that Miz has had. At every turn, he has far exceeded the expectations we have shaped for him. Why should his place on this list be any different? A dissection of the data will show that he should also not be misconstrued as a Ziggler of Kofi type. Miz has a legitimate resume if you can get past that he's The Miz and he's not quite as awesome to a lot of fans as he is to himself. One of his Tag Team Championship reigns with John Morrison was the 6th longest of the WrestleMania Era and he has 553 total days as a Tag titleholder. When he graduated to the United States Championship, he had a single reign of 7 ½ months and 436 total days as holder of either the US or the Intercontinental Championship. As WWE Champion – remember, the *WWE Champion* and not the World Title passed around to experimentals – Miz main-evented WrestleMania en route to a 160 day reign – the 5th longest WWE Title reign of the decade as of late summer 2015. Like him or not, Miz has had a golden career.

#20: Jeff Jarrett

4-time WCW World Heavyweight Champion; 6-time WWE Intercontinental Champion; 3-time WCW United States Champion; 1-time WWE Tag Team Champion

If there is a career that has been more inexplicably underrated than Jeff Jarrett's in the WrestleMania Era, then please write me and let me know. I suppose it is because Double J won the WCW Championship four times during the worst creative period in mainstream pro wrestling history, but I think that perhaps there are other, better historical perspectives in which Jarrett's run at the top should be placed. Many may not remember just how awful the WCW main-event scene was from the standpoint of in-ring quality. It was atrocious during the height of the Monday Night War. Men like Jarrett, Booker T, Scott Steiner, and Bret Hart rescued it from the depths of despair and they may not have drawn the ratings or buyrates that did the New World Order, but wrestling is not just about getting butts in the seats or eyes on the screen – it's also about putting on a good enough show that those butts and eyes become repeat viewers and buyers. So, as I strongly suggested in *The WrestleMania Era*, celebrate the incredible career of Jeff Jarrett – not only a four-time World Champion, but also a three-time United States Champion and former Tag Team Champion and the wrestler that has held the Intercontinental Title more times than anyone but Chris Jericho.

#19: Shawn Michaels

4-time WWE World Heavyweight Champion; 3-time WWE
Intercontinental Champion; 5-time WWE Tag Team Champion

Earning the tie-breaker to get to #19 ahead of Jarrett on
account of his holding the World Title for a year longer in
totality, Shawn Michaels breaks into the Top 20 of the all-time
greatest champions despite never really cashing in on the fact
that two World Championships were up for grabs during the last
eight years of his career. The opportunity was there for a
substantial amount of stat-padding from 2002-2010, but just a
pair of short Tag Team Championship reigns and the lone
additional World Heavyweight Championship run that made up
just a few weeks of his overall 14 months as the top titleholder
were all that Michaels added to his considerable 1990s resume.
I'd call that pretty impressive. For a lot of HBK's peers in the
second halves of their careers, the Brand Extension in the 2000s
was to their championship track records what WCW had been
for the top guys of the 1980s – a method / place to strengthen
their legacies. Michaels was the rare star to headline PPVs
repeatedly, but further his legacy through the strength of his
performances without the assistance of a lot of gold around his
waist. The bulk of HBK's stellar trophy case was built from
1992-1997. Take out his twilight run and he's still in the Top 25.

#18: Batista

6-time WWE World Heavyweight Champion; 4-time WWE Tag
Team Champion

Batista was also involved in the three-way tie for #20,
but gets the boost to 18th all-time via holding the World
Championship for 120 days longer than HBK. His limited
number of other championship accolades (and paltry 113 days
combined over four reigns as Tag Team Champion) should speak
to how dominant a World Champion Batista really was. He only
held the WWE Championship for 37 days in two short reigns,

but if we were to measure a wrestler's worth by the lengthiest of his title reigns, Batista was certainly worth a lot to WWE. The Animal was the longest single reigning World Heavyweight Champion in WWE history – and one of the top 15 longest single reigning champions of the last 25 years; he and his mentor, Triple H, share the spotlight as the pinnacles of achievement for that title's 11 year run, with Batista narrowly edging Hunter for longest average time as champion across multiple title reigns (126 day average over 4 reigns versus 123 day average over 5 reigns). I always admired about Big Dave that he took seriously the role of being "The Man" in an outward expression of his position, even though history would show John Cena to have taken that moniker from him before he'd ever truly earned it. His place on this list, earned almost solely through World Championships, reflects that.

#17: Lex Luger

2-time WCW World Heavyweight Champion; 5-time NWA/WCW United States Champion; 3-time NWA/WCW Tag Team Champion

Many like to claim that, as of the late 1980s, the Intercontinental Championship was the second most important title in all of professional wrestling. Given that it was so prominently featured at *WrestleManias III, V,* and *VI* and how gigantic a lead WWE had built in their competition with WCW, that might be true, but a strong argument could be made for the NWA/WCW World Title too. We need to be sure, though, amidst the argument for which was the second grandest prize of that era, not to forget about the importance of the NWA/WCW United States Championship; and for one reason: Lex Luger. In another perfect example of "the man making the title," Luger ensured that the US Title was very much relevant in the championship prestige conversation. The Total Package was nothing less than one of the Top 5 stars in the business back then and it was during that time that he amassed the majority of his 948 total days as US Champ, making him the most successful US or IC champion of all-time. Sans for the 50 days that Stan Hansen was champion, Lex Luger held the US Title for over two years between May 1989 and July 1991 - when he vacated the belt after becoming World Heavyweight Champion.

#16: The Big Show

4-time WWE World Heavyweight Champion; 2-time WCW World Heavyweight Champion; 1-time WWE Intercontinental Champion; 1-time WWE United States Champion; 3-time WCW Tag Team Champion; 6-time WWE Tag Team Champion

If the argument for greatest super heavyweight of all-time between Big Show, Andre, Vader, Undertaker, Kane, and Bam Bam Bigelow could be settled on the strength of their championship accolades, then it is the World's Largest Athlete who would get the nod, narrowly edging out the Deadman. Does anyone else find it fascinating that some of the biggest wrestlers ever have had the longest careers? Taker, Kane, and Show have all been around for 20 years and counting. It would be easy to assume that the larger the talent, the faster he would physically break down. Alas, here Show sits as the most successful champion of his super heavyweight peers, having won every title that there is to win in WWE and was to win in WCW. He actually holds the distinction as the youngest World Heavyweight Champion ever. Randy Orton is blessed with that moniker for his WWE achievement, but Show was younger when he first won the title in WCW. He never reigned for very long as a singles champion, holding the World Title for 268 days combined and the IC or US Titles for just 175 total days, but he did amass an impressive Tag Team Championship resume with 9 reigns for 542 days. Only a handful of wrestlers have ever held the Tag Team Titles for longer.

#15: "Macho Man" Randy Savage

2-time WWE Champion; 4-time WCW World Heavyweight Champion; 1-time WWE Intercontinental Champion

With just seven total championships in his career, it would seem that "Macho Man" was a big enough title to keep Randy Savage so relevant in this discussion. As big a star as he was, particularly in WWE, he would win titles and hang onto them for quite awhile. Long reigns are the great equalizer when a wrestler is placed against peers whose golden trophy cases are fuller. Savage held his singles championships for nearly a combined 1,000 days. Part of that was a by-product of his era, but certainly a lot of it had to do with how awesome he was too. It was his reputation that was largely responsible for the stat-padding he was able to accumulate with 4 short reigns as WCW Champion. When you consider that those reigns combined to last just 53 days, the fact that he is still one of the Top 10 longest reigning World Champions of the WrestleMania Era on the back of his 2 stints as WWE Champion becomes all the more impressive. He also still ranks as one of the Top 10 longest reigning Intercontinental Champions despite having held the strap just once. Of the five categories that shape the overall *WrestleMania Era* list, the Title Factor was Macho Man's weakest...and he's still the 15th greatest champion. One of the G.O.A.Ts for sure.

#14: Chris Benoit

1-time WWE World Heavyweight Champion; 1-time WCW World Heavyweight Champion; 4-time WWE Intercontinental Champion; 5-time WCW/WWE United States Champion; 4-time WWE Tag Team Champion; 2-time WCW Tag Team Champion

In *The WrestleMania Era*, I made the conscious decision to nullify much of Chris Benoit's statistical achievements as my personal way of accepting the fact that history should not necessarily reflect on his career the way it would have if he had not done what he did at the end of his life. I still put him in the Top 30 because I think it's important that we account for the wrestler's career in the midst of condemning the man for heinous actions. On this list, there's no Doc-imposed qualifier.

Chris Benoit was simply the 14th greatest champion of the modern era of professional wrestling. He's one of the most decorated champions ever, having accumulated almost 20 major titles. He is one of the top 10 United States Champions of all-time by total length of reigns. On the merit of his hard work and dedication to his craft, he won the World Heavyweight Championship in both WCW and WWE. So, there should be no questioning or qualifying such an objective statistic as championship glory. Given what he accomplished despite his size and minimal personality, he should remain – quietly – one of the most inspirational stories in wrestling lore; his career merits that.

#13: Sting

7-time NWA/WCW World Heavyweight Champion; 2-time WCW United States Champion; 3-time WCW Tag Team Champion

Among the former champions who never won a title in WWE, Sting ranks the highest; he was also the only predominantly WCW wrestler to crack the overall Top 15 of *The WrestleMania Era*. It's true that in many ways he *was* WCW; his championship resume reflects that – 12 titles, all in WCW, still good for 13th greatest of the WrestleMania Era. I'd call that a stellar accomplishment and one of the reasons why WCW history needs to be more heavily considered in discussions about the greatest ever.

It was not just the titles listed that made him such a decorated champion, but the consistency across the board with which he held those championships. Of the wrestlers listed thus far, only Sting and Shawn Michaels held the World Title for at least 400 days, the US or IC Title for at least 200 days, and the Tag Team Titles for at least 200 days. That's an elite club (the 400-200-200 club) that will gain a few more members before all is said and done here; to have achieved it in one promotion is astounding. The Franchise, indeed, Sting truly was...

#12: Stone Cold Steve Austin

6-time WWE Champion; 2-time WWE Intercontinental Champion; 2-time WCW United States Champion; 4-time WWE Tag Team Champion; 1-time WCW Tag Team Champion

Stone Cold is the first member of the 500-300-300 club, thanks in part to splitting time in WCW and WWE. History has, perhaps, had a tendency to forget about Austin's time in Ted Turner's promotion. In WCW, he held the US and Tag Team Championships long enough to boost the statistical value of his career. WWE, then, served the purpose of skyrocketing Austin up the historical ladder. He became the rare talent to complete the WWE Triple Crown in less than a year, winning the Tag Team Championship and Intercontinental Championship during the spring/summer of 1997 and winning the WWE Championship at the following year's WrestleMania. He became the second man to hold the WWE Title for at least six times during the course of his dominant run as the top star in the industry. Take away WCW, though, and Austin isn't nearly as successful a champion. The bulk of his mid-card title success came from WCW, his tag team with Brian Pillman accounting for over half of his days as co-holder of the Tag Team Titles and his impressive run with the United States Title making up most of his 309 days as a mid-card singles champion. "Stunning" Steve may not have been anywhere near as successful as "Stone Cold" Steve, but the Hollywood Blonde part of his career was important.

#11: Kevin "Diesel" Nash

1-time WWE Champion; 5-time WCW World Heavyweight Champion; 1-time WWE Intercontinental Champion; 2-time WWE Tag Team Champion; 9-time WCW Tag Team Champion

The record for shortest amount of time (from debut to accomplishment) needed to complete WWE's Triple Crown is held by none other than Kevin Nash, who might well have the most balanced resume of any wrestler in history. WWE likes to celebrate that Diesel won the Triple Crown in his first year with the company; I'd like to point out that he actually did in a little over half a year. It was that feat which set the tone for the rest of his highly decorated career. He was the longest reigning WWE Champion of the 1990s with 358 days as titleholder. He well balanced that extremely long run on top with five reigns as WCW Champion that would make DDP and Mick Foley blush for their brevity. What most people don't realize is that Nash is the 3rd longest reigning Tag Team Champion of the WrestleMania Era behind only Billy Gunn and Kane. I heard from some fans prior to the WWE Hall of Fame ceremony in 2015 who scoffed at Nash being the headliner of the class; I scoffed back at them for failing to realize how awesome a career that Diesel had amassed between WWE and WCW. You take all the influential things that he did during the Monday Night War and combine them with his championship accolades and you have nothing less than a Hall of Fame class headliner's resume.

#10: Chris Jericho

6-time WWE World Heavyweight Champion; 9-time WWE Intercontinental Champion; 5-time WWE Tag Team Champion

Our countdown from ten to one begins with Chris Jericho. When we think of championships and Y2J, naturally we first think of his becoming the first ever Undisputed Champion in December 2001; he has also held the Intercontinental Championship more times than any peer. In that respect, his place in the Top 10 is welcomed with open arms. However, the fact that his major singles championship track record includes average World Heavyweight and Intercontinental Title reigns of 35 and 36 days, respectively, brings to the forefront the debate at the heart of this entire project: is it more prestigious to have won a lot of championships held for shorter periods of time or to have won fewer championships held over longer periods of time? Jericho has never been one to care about length of reign, citing his first (unofficial) run with the WWE Championship that lasted for half a Monday Night Raw as a career highlight that segued to future World Title wins. Should it matter that, of the Top 25 Champions of the WrestleMania Era, he held the World Championship for the fifth fewest number of days? Or should it matter he won the World Championship six times? Frankly, both should matter. Greatness implies magnitude, but vastness can be defined by long title reigns *and* many title reigns.

#9: The Rock
10-time WWE World Heavyweight Champion; 2-time WWE Intercontinental Champion; 5-time WWE Tag Team Champion

When it comes to greatness, perhaps nobody in pro wrestling lore eclipses Dwayne "The Rock" Johnson. The Rock made himself "The Great *One*" on the back of his Intercontinental Championship success in 1997 and 1998 followed by his emergence as the 1A of the Attitude Era to Steve Austin. He remains the longest reigning IC Champion of the modern era, his 265 day reign having no peers since it wrapped up in a Ladder match loss to Triple H at *Summerslam '98*. That success translated well to the main-event scene, where he captured the World Heavyweight Championship on ten different occasions. The Rock joins Hulk Hogan and The Undertaker as the only men to have held the World Title in three separate decades. His 464 total days as the top champion, which are just a month greater than CM Punk's modern day record *single* reign, may not exactly set the world on fire with their average across ten reigns, but there should be no questioning that the People's Champ did well for himself. His Tag Team Championship success, however, is almost laughable. He held the straps five times for a combined 24 days – the worst average (under 5 days per reign) of any wrestler with a comparable number of Tag Titles.

#8: Randy Orton

12-time WWE World Heavyweight Champion; 1-time WWE Intercontinental Champion; 1-time WWE Tag Team Champion

The other prominent third generation wrestler to grace the Top 10, Randy Orton followed a similar wrestling career path as The Rock. The Intercontinental Championship was the first title that Orton won and, since Rock's 265 day reign ended in August '98, the Viper is the 3rd longest reigning IC titleholder with a 210 day run that spanned from *Armageddon '03* to *Vengeance '04*. His lone Tag Team Championship alongside Edge in the underrated faction Rated RKO was the only other title that Orton held besides the World Title. It has basically been main-event or bust for the Apex Predator for most of his career. Like his heralded fellow OVW '02 classmate, John Cena, Orton has been a fixture in the World Title picture, competing for it on PPV every year since his first title shot at *Summerslam 2004*. The two of them have set the current standard for sustained main-eventing. Orton is three World Title victories back from Cena's fifteen total and just one behind his mentor, Triple H. Those three rank 2nd, 3rd, and 4th all-time in total World Championships. Though he ranks 8th overall among the greatest champions, Orton ranks 5th in the WrestleMania Era for combined number of days as World Champion (747 days). History will one day greatly appreciate the accomplishments of Randy Orton.

#7: Booker T

1-time WWE World Heavyweight Champion; 5-time WCW World Heavyweight Champion; 1-time WWE Intercontinental Champion; 4-time WCW/WWE United States Champion; 3-time WWE Tag Team Champion; 11-time WCW Tag Team Champion

When I ranked Booker T outside of the Top 30 of *The WrestleMania Era* in my book, I knew that some people would note the championship track record that I cited in the appendix, see that he's the 7th most accomplished champion of the last 30+ years and scoff that he was not a 1st Tier selection. That's a valid complaint and the response serves as a reminder that these discussions of overall greatness need to be more complex than they've generally been. The fact remains that Booker T won more championships than anyone in WCW history. He initially made his name as a tag team wrestler and is currently the most decorated Tag Team Champion ever (WWE and WCW combined) with fourteen reigns. He arrived in WWE as a 5-time WCW Champion and United States Champion and never slowed down, adding eight more titles to his overall collection.

It is noteworthy to point out that Book's singles title reign lengths are a bit deceiving. The numbers are solid – 379 as World Champ and 305 days as a mid-card champion – but they are skewed by his becoming the WCW World and WCW US Champion right as WCW was closing its doors, giving him title reigns that technically count despite being off television and never defended for several months in early 2001 (the same phenomenon that aided The Natural Born Thrillers being placed higher on the list).

#6: Bret Hart
5-time WWE Champion; 2-time WCW Champion; 2-time WWE Intercontinental Champion; 5-time WCW/WWE United States Champion; 2-time WWE Tag Team Champion; 1-time WCW Tag Team Champion

Ranking about a month behind Randy Orton for 6th longest reigning World Champion of the WrestleMania Era, Bret Hart has clearly stamped his overall candidacy for the ever-to-remain-growing list of all-time top stars. A few pages back, praise was given to Batista for the seriousness with which he took the responsibility of being champion – of being "The Man." Perhaps nobody ever took that role more seriously than Bret. Some would even say that he took it too seriously, but that's beside the point; and the point is clear: Bret "Hitman" Hart is one of the greatest champions ever, bar none, and the fact that it meant so much to him had a tendency to make it mean more to fans when he was the champion. As a two-time Tag Team Champion who reigned for over 16 months in WWE (it took Booker T 14 reigns to garner just one month longer as a titleholder), Bret was proud to be the face of the tag team division with his brother-in-law. As a two-time Intercontinental Champion, Bret set a standard that inspired many young wrestlers. As a 5-time WWE Champion, Bret was responsible for ushering in an era for the main-event scene that was predicated upon excellent execution on the 20'X20' canvas. There were also the WCW accolades that padded his stats as he added their Triple Crown to his resume after inventing the concept in WWE. There may never be another Bret Hart, folks...

#5: Edge
11-time WWE World Heavyweight Champion; 5-time WWE Intercontinental Champion; 1-time WCW United States Champion; 13-time WWE Tag Team Champion

My name is Chad Matthews and I'm an Edgehead. When I wrote *The WrestleMania Era*, I anticipated a lot of disgruntlement about some of my Top 10 placements, where Andre the Giant was ranked, and a handful of other decisions. I did not anticipate that #11 of the Top 90 would be one of the most frequent topics of derision. Good Lord, folks...look at Edge's resume. If we attempt to objectify as best we can wrestling's all-time greatest, why would anyone be surprised that the most decorated champion in WWE history would rank so highly overall? Thirty major titles! Across the board, Edge is a statistically dominant force in sports entertainment lore, with his championship resume being the shining achievement. 5[Th] all-time; an absolutely incredible mark for the kid who once sat in the crowd at *WrestleMania VI*, geeking out like all of us do.

Last year, Edge and Christian joined Steve Austin for a WWE Network episode of the Stone Cold podcast and – maybe this is just my interpretation – it seemed that the Rattlesnake was subtly questioning the Ultimate Opportunist's place among the pantheon. Christian did his best to squash any doubt, immediately calling his best friend "one of the greatest of all-time." Of course he is. I wonder if there will come a day when it doesn't seem like Edge fans have to defend his status as a first-ballot Hall of Famer.

#4: Triple H
13-time WWE World Heavyweight Champion; 5-time WWE Intercontinental Champion; 2-time WWE Tag Team Champion

The Top 4 greatest champions of the WrestleMania Era are the only four members of the WrestleMania Era's 1,000 day World Champion club. Triple H was the champion of the world for 1,155 days across his third all-time 13 reigns from 1999 to 2009. The Game's 280 day initial reign as the *Raw* brand's World Heavyweight Champion was the longest single reign since Diesel's year-long run from November '94 to November '95. He had another 200+ day reign from 2008 to 2009. Nine of his reigns, however, failed to last longer than three months. He, therefore, was involved in the trend that saw the World Championship passed around frequently, much to his statistical advantage, and he was also essentially responsible for bringing back the trend of long-reigning champions.

As was brought to the forefront in the HBK chapter, The Monday Night War afforded the stars from the 80s and 90s a chance to further fill their golden trophy cases across two companies and the Brand Extension gave stars from the 2000s a chance to do the same across two shows; Triple H embodies the latter opportunity and its inherent advantages, statistically.

#3: Hulk Hogan
6-time WWE Champion; 6-time WCW Champion; 1-time WWE Tag Team Champion

Hulk Hogan is the first of two members of the 3,000 day World Championship club in the WrestleMania Era. A six-time World Champion in both WWE and WCW, he is ahead of Triple H by a good distance using the Title Formula, making the race for greatest champion of the WrestleMania Era between just three horses. If you read through his resume, you'll note a distinct lack of non-World Titles. That lone, brief Tag Team Championship reign with Edge was an anomaly; Hulk Hogan entered the WrestleMania Era as a main-eventer and never stopped being one. Considering that he dominated the 1980s in WWE and dominated the 1990s in WCW, it would be difficult to call his non-stop headliner status a disadvantage. This conversation between him and his Top 3 peers is the one exception. Momentarily, you'll see that the only two men who rank ahead of Hogan had considerable depth added to their title resumes by mid-card runs; one was even aided by a twilight run that saw him drop down the pecking order. There was never any dropping down on any superstar hierarchy for Hulk Hogan.

The Hulkster was the longest reigning World Champion since *Starrcade '83*. 3,362 days, folks. That means that 30% of the WrestleMania Era featured Hulk Hogan as the World Champion. If that figure is ever equaled over 30+ years, I'll be shocked.

#2: John Cena

15-time WWE World Heavyweight Champion; 5-time WWE United States Champion; 4-time WWE Tag Team Champion

The modern era does have its advantages, statistically; that has been made very clear. Less apprehension toward making a title change is one of the key differences between the first and second halves of the WrestleMania Era. Another is that there are so many special shows (PPVs), allowing wrestlers like John Cena to accumulate a gigantic amount of headlining matches and, with them, a greater number of chances to critically shine. There's also the Wellness Policy, which forces wrestlers to be smarter about their health – that's something that will likely extend many a career and allow for further title accumulation and main-event stats and even the playing field to a degree despite their being just one World Championship. Cena is the poster child for these benefits.

The Golden Boy is a statistical beast. He's the third longest reigning World Champion of the last thirty years, with 1,394 days atop WWE with the gold around his waist. Add to that his year and counting as the United States Champion across five reigns and he's unquestionably the top titleholder of his generation and the pacesetter for future generations to come. Hogan and Flair had advantages too, the most obvious being the penchant for promotions to keep their titles on one guy consistently for such long stretches. Cena ranking ahead of Hogan and being in position to one day catch Flair – another four month or longer reign as WWE Champion would not just tie Flair for the once-thought-impossible-to-duplicate 16-time World Champion mark, but would also pull him even with Flair as the greatest champion of the last thirty-plus years.

#1: Ric Flair

14-time NWA/WCW World Heavyweight Champion; 2-time WWE Champion; 1-time WWE Intercontinental Champion; 1-time WCW United States Champion; 3-time WWE Tag Team Champion

*This is a good time to offer a final reminder that only reigns from the WrestleMania Era (*Starrcade '83* to the present) were considered for this list; it should be noted that if every wrestler's pre-Nov. 1983 stats were reinstated, Flair would win this competition by an astounding 34 points using the Title Formula. Please see the appendix to fully appreciate that*

The above point is vitally important to contextualizing Ric Flair's status as the greatest champion of the last thirty years. If you account for his overall resume and add back in his NWA World Tag Team Championship and NWA United States Championship reigns, then the Nature Boy is far and away the most successful titleholder of anyone who participated in the WrestleMania Era. That point only serves to emphasize just how incredible a career that Flair had. You can take away his mid-card success that made him such a viable candidate to become NWA World Heavyweight Champion, WWE Champion, and WCW Champion for over 3,000 days and he still has a reasonably comfortable lead on his next closest competitor for the top spot. Flair is our Hank Aaron or Kareem Abdul-Jabbar. No matter if he is overtaken by Cena as the greatest champion of modern times, he will forever and always be in the argument for greatest ever, period. His record number of reigns as the World Champion will someday be equaled and it will someday be exceeded too, but his influence as a champion who was so impassioned about professional wrestling will only be someday equaled; it will never be exceeded.

WOOOOO!